CONTENTS

1 Introducing Mauritius

Like a rich green emerald, swathed in the translucent, turquoise silk of the southwest Indian Ocean, Mauritius is a small island which has only recently, since the early 1980s, made a sizeable impact on world tourism. Only 67km (42 miles) in length and 46km (29 miles) at its widest point, and with an area of 1865km² (730 sq miles), it is about the size of the English county of Surrey, or South Africa's Cape Peninsula and False Bay.

As a political entity, the Republic of Mauritius includes not only the island of Mauritius itself, set just north of the Tropic of Capricorn at 20°S and 58°E, but also the tiny island of Rodrigues some 563km (350 miles) to the east, as well as the Cargados Carajos Archipelago (St Brandon) and the two virtually uninhabited Agalega islands, 400km (250 miles) to the northeast and 1000km (620 miles) to the north of Mauritius respectively.

The warm climate and the blue-green sea gently lapping the sandy shores within the protective belt of the coral reef make for a tropical paradise with equally warm people whose friendliness is legendary. Indeed, the motto most people who know the island will associate with Mauritius is the easy-going 'No problem'. Nothing is too much of a problem for these hospitable islanders, whose roots reach back in history to India, Madagascar, East Africa, China, France and England. With this rich mix of cultures and a population of just over a million people, Mauritians have realized that the only viable option in the small area of this island is peaceful coexistence.

Top Attractions

Soaking up the sun on a white, sandy beach.
Water sports of every kind – snorkelling, diving, sailing, windsurfing, and parasailing.
Big-game fishing in first-rate fishing waters.
Scuba diving amidst coral gardens and tropical fish.
Nature walks – mountains, gorges and waterfalls.
Gastronomy – a rich mix of culinary delights; seafood plays a major part.
Shopping – especially wooden model boats, jewellery, clothing and flowers.

Opposite: *A yacht heads past Trou aux Biches.*

THE LAND

Mauritius owes its origins to volcanic activity. Although the volcanoes are long since dormant, they have left their mark on the profile and landscape of the island, notably in the striking forms of some of the mountain peaks in the west and in the several volcanic craters found on the island. From the north coast the land rises gradually to the highest parts of the island: once possibly the floor of a gigantic crater, the central plateau now reaches a height of 580m (1903ft) and is edged by four mountain ranges – the Moka Range encircling Port Louis, the Bambous Mountains in the east and the Black River and Savanne ranges in the southwest. From the central plain the land descends more sharply to the south coast. With the high rainfall of the interior, numerous small rivers cut through the landscape to the coast.

Sugar-cane plantations once covered much of Mauritius, and while this crop is no longer the main earner of foreign exchange, rolling fields of cane are still the prevailing feature in many parts of the island.

Although **Port Louis**, in the northwest, is the capital of Mauritius and the centre of business activity, the majority of those who work there prefer to live in the relative coolness of the nearby towns and suburbs of the plateau, such as **Quatre Bornes**, **Curepipe**, **Rose Hill/Beau Bassin** and **Vacoas/Phoenix**. The only other sizable town is **Mahébourg** in the southeast; the remaining settlements studding the coastline are largely tourist resorts or fishing villages.

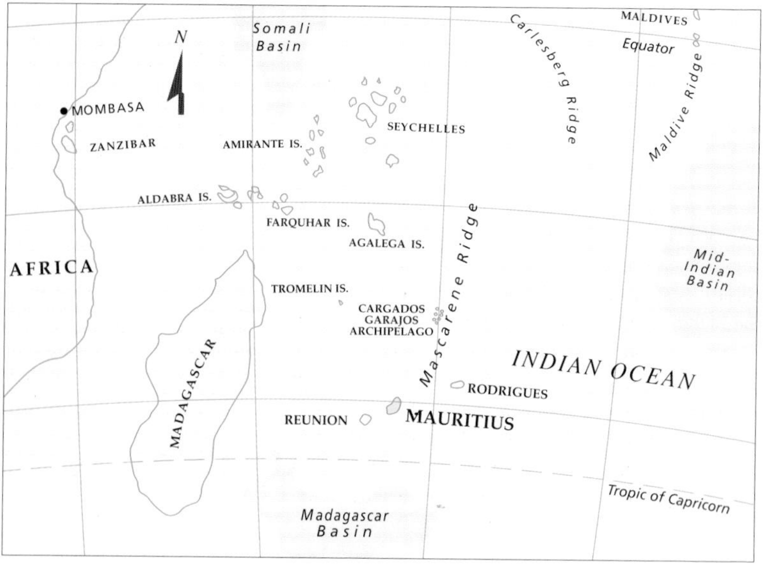

Mountains and Rivers

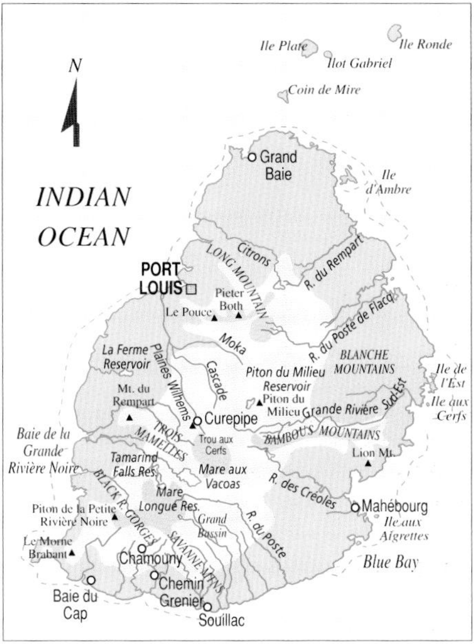

Not surprisingly, the mountains on this small island in the middle of the ocean do not rise to great heights, though many are unusual in form. The highest is **le Piton de la Petite Rivière Noire** in the southwest, at 828m (2717ft), closely followed in height by the **Pieter Both** (823m; 2700ft), towering over Port Louis, with its steep shoulders surmounted by a bobble of rock. Also rising above the capital is **le Pouce**, or 'the thumb'.

The mountains running down the western side of the island include **le Corps de Garde**, overlooking Rose Hill (which some say got its name from the light of sunrise on the mountain); **le Rempart**, like a small-scale Matterhorn in appearance; and the dramatically steep and pointed formation of **les Trois Mamelles**, which no doubt earned its name from the udder-like shape of its three peaks.

On the southwest tip of the island lies **le Morne Brabant**, last mountainous outcrop of this rugged region. Although not particularly high, this mountain is quite dramatic with its rocky cliff face dropping away to the low-lying land of le Morne peninsula. It can easily be climbed and offers spectacular views of the southwest corner of Mauritius. **Le Piton du Milieu**, in the centre of the island, offers the intrepid climber a view of almost the entire island. **La Montagne du Lion** is a spur of the Bambous Mountains in the southeast; its form, the profile of a lion lying down, dominates views of Mahébourg.

Mauritius' island neighbour of Réunion, part of the Mascarene Archipelago, can still boast volcanic activity, but the only obvious evidence of Mauritius' fiery past lies in the craters of Trou Kanaka, Grand Bassin and Bassin Blanc in the south, and Trou aux Cerfs at Curepipe.

Facts and Figures

- **Highest mountain** is the Piton de la Rivière Noire at 828m (2717ft); it overlooks the settlement of Rivière Noire in the southwest of the island.
- **Longest river** is la Grande Rivière Sud-Est at 34km (21 miles) in length; it empties into the sea on the east side of the island.
- **Biggest waterfall** is the Tamarind Falls, with a total drop of 295m (968ft), in the west of the island.
- **Strangest physical feature** is the coloured volcanic earths at Chamarel which are said to separate naturally into seven colours when a sample is shaken.

Above: *The dramatic colours of the lagoon at Ile aux Cerfs on the east coast.*

Grande Rivière Sud-Est, which runs into the sea near Ile aux Cerfs, is the longest of the many rivers and streams that wend their way across the island; some, such as the **Rivière Noire** or **Black River**, cut through the land to form gorges of breathtaking beauty.

Seas and Shores

The 160km (99 mile) coastline is almost entirely fringed by coral reefs, and consequently the coastal waters mainly lie in calm lagoons. On the landward side these are bordered by crescents of white coral sand, thanks to the gradual erosion of the reefs, and casuarinas dominate the tropical vegetation. It is only really in the south, where the reef drops away, that the marine landscape becomes less placid; here, strong currents and rocky shores render the waters unsafe for water sports.

A number of small islands are dotted here and there just off the coast of Mauritius, among which are the unusual wedge-shaped **Coin de Mire**, visible from most places on the northern coastline, **Ile Ronde** (Round Island) and **Ile Plate** (Flat Island), also to the north, both of which harbour indigenous birds and flora. Some of them can be visited on day trips catering for scuba exploration, nature study or simply picnics. **Ile aux Cerfs** in the east offers 7km (4 miles) of casuarina-

Climatic Extremes

- The **wettest** part of the island is in Curepipe which receives nearly 3m (10ft) of rain a year.
- The **driest** side of the island is the west coast, which receives only 670mm (26in) of rain annually and needs irrigation for its sugar-cane plantations.
- The **hottest** part of the island is the west coast with temperatures reaching daily highs of 31°C (88°F) or more.
- The **coolest** is on the central plateau with maximum temperatures reaching not more than 27°C (81°F).
- The **windiest** weather is experienced on the east coast in winter.

fringed coastline, making it a tropical island paradise. Other islands of interest include **Ile d'Ambre**, which can be visited on daily excursions, and **Ile aux Aigrettes**, where a visitors centre has opened.

All beaches are officially public, although access from the road to the sea is sometimes restricted where hotels and private bungalows have been built; some hotels post guards at the beach restricting entry, although they have no legal right to do so. Most of the accessible beaches have toilet facilities, picnic sites and sometimes kiosks selling snacks and souvenirs. They are just as good as those in front of the hotels, though they tend to be crowded over weekends, particularly on Sundays, and on public holidays.

Climate

The **seasons** can be divided broadly into a hot, wet season, lasting from December to April, and a pleasantly cool, dry season from May to November, making Mauritius a year-round tourist destination.

Maximum summer coastal **temperatures** average 33°C (91°F) and winters average 24°C (75°F) – usually about 5C° (9F°) warmer than the higher interior. The coolest months are July, August and September, but even at this time the sea water is warm and most enjoyable, with a temperature of not less than 20°C (68°F).

The **rainy months** are between January and May but rainfall is usually higher in the centre of the island. The west coast, extending from the Rivière Noire area up to Port Louis, has a hotter, drier environment than the more isolated east coast, which is blessed by the southeasterly trade winds blowing onshore and providing a welcome breeze as a respite from the summer heat. In winter, however, they are much stronger.

Cyclones are active in this corner of the Indian Ocean from January through to April. Some years, cyclones miss the island altogether or are very mild, while at other times they can be devastating, destroying buildings

COMPARATIVE CLIMATE CHART	**PORT LOUIS**				**MAHEBOURG**				**CUREPIPE**			
	SUM JAN	AUT APR	WIN JULY	SPR OCT	SUM JAN	AUT APR	WIN JULY	SPR OCT	SUM JAN	AUT APR	WIN JULY	SPR OCT
MAX TEMP. °C	31	30	26	26	29	28	24	26	26	24	20	23
MIN TEMP. °C	24	23	19	20	23	22	20	19	19	18	14	15
MAX TEMP. °F	88	87	79	83	85	83	75	80	78	75	68	73
MIN TEMP. °F	75	73	66	68	73	71	68	66	67	65	57	59
HOURS SUN	8	7	7	8	7	6	6	7	8	6	6	7
RAINFALL in	7	3	1	4	11	11	5	3	13	11	8	4
RAINFALL mm	165	87	20	18	282	232	135	80	328	292	194	104

CYCLONES

Devastating cyclones have hit Mauritius periodically throughout its history. In 1867, a cyclone killed half the people of Port Louis, and 25 years later another caused the loss of over 1000 lives and destroyed almost all the island's crops. More recently Cyclone Carol on 25 February 1960, with a gust speed of up to 256kph (159mph), killed 40 people, left 80,000 homeless and destroyed 70,000 buildings. Cyclone Jenny on 27 February 1962 had a maximum gust speed of 275kph (171mph); Gervaise on 5 February 1975 gusted up to 278kph (173mph); Claudette on 21 December 1979 buffeted the island with gusts of up to 256kph (159mph). The most recent cyclone, Davina, ripped through the island in March 1999.

and vegetation. In February 1999, Mauritius witnessed one of the driest cyclones of all times. Although the island is vulnerable, cyclones are not an annual event. Even so, most hotels are well fortified against the ravages of cyclones, and have their own generators in case of power failure.

Plant Life

Exotic and brilliantly colourful **fruits** and **flowers** thrive in the island's tropical climate. Purple-flowering jacarandas, 60 different species of orchid, pink, red and white anthuriums, the sweetly perfumed frangipani, scarlet flamboyant, pink cassia, lilac, bougainvillea in brilliant purples, reds and pinks, hibiscus and cannas are all part of the lush vegetation bedecking the island.

Among **tropical fruits**, bananas, pineapples and to some extent papayas can be found all year round; guavas, mangoes and litchis are more seasonal. December is the best month for fruit and at Christmas many Mauritians enjoy a pineapple, litchi and mango salad – to which some add a pinch of salt and some sliced chillis! The island's main crop is still sugar cane, which once covered some 80% of the arable land.

Over 1000 plants are indigenous to Mauritius, of which about 300 are truly unique. However, the majority of the plant species were introduced on the island in the last 300 years by various settlers.

Below: *Coconut palms, the ubiquitous tropical plant.*
Opposite: *The sheer vibrancy of Mauritius' abundant flora.*

The **teak**, **ebony** and ***colophane* forests** which once covered Mauritius proved an irresistible attraction for the early Dutch and French colonists, who overexploited the island's arboreal heritage. Forests were also removed to make way for sugar-cane plantations; today indigenous forest covers less than 1% of the island's surface and is concentrated mainly in the Black River Gorges National Park in the southwest. Some of the few remaining *colophane* trees are said to be around 1000 years old. The most commonly seen tree now is the **casuarina**, a pine-like tree known locally as the *filao*, which was introduced in 1778 and planted around the coastline because of its ability to grow near salt water. It also acts as a

windbreak and provides shade. Other common trees here include the **banyan** or ***multipliant***, a large, spreading tree with aerial roots that grow towards the ground, forever seeking new places to take root; and the **traveller's palm**, a tree with foliage like that of the banana tree, and flowers that resemble strelitzias.

GARDENS AND NATURE RESERVES

- The **Sir Seewoosagur Ramgoolam Botanic Garden**, Pamplemousses
- **Curepipe Botanical Gardens**
- **Company Gardens**, Port Louis city centre
- **Robert Edward Hart Gardens,** south side of Port Louis harbour
- **Balfour Municipal Garden**, Beau Bassin
- **Le Réduit** – formal garden in a tropical setting
- **Creole Museum**, Eurêka – magnificent gardens with views of the waterfalls of the Moka River
- **Plaine Champagne** and the **Black River Gorges** – with their many indigenous plants and animals
- **Le Domaine du Chasseur** near Mahébourg – 1500ha (3700 acres) of forest-covered mountainside.

Animal Kingdom

Mauritius' most notable contribution to the world's natural history gallery of extinct creatures is the dodo, whose presence was first recorded by the Dutch in 1681; by 1692 this large, flightless bird had been hunted to extinction. The solitaire, a relative of the dodo, was likewise made extinct by settlers on Rodrigues. Giant tortoises and turtles also fell victim to the excesses of the settlers, while the Mauritian branches of various other bird families died out; the only rare and indigenous **birds** still in existence today and of significance to naturalists are the pink pigeon, the Mauritius kestrel and the echo parakeet. Despite this, Mauritius is richly endowed with bird life – sparrows, weaver birds, Indian mynahs, paradise flycatchers, red cardinals, various doves, and the *paille-en-queue* or tropic bird all abound on the island, having been introduced from other parts of the world over the last 400 years, while the coastline is frequented by several kinds of tern.

The island has only one indigenous **mammal** – the Mauritius fruit bat or golden bat. Monkeys, hares and deer also exist in the wild, the latter having been introduced by the Dutch settlers in the 17th century from Java, while mongooses were brought from India at the turn of this century to control the rats which were overrunning the cane fields.

There are no poisonous **reptiles** on the island. The only snakes are the *couleuvre* or Indian wolf snake which was imported from India, and two species of boa constrictor found on Ile Ronde. This small island is also home to the endemic Telfair skink.

The Dodo

The name of this large, ungainly bird came from the Portuguese *duodo* or *deodar*, meaning 'stupid'. It survived on hard seeds and grains, hence the shape of its beak; to digest them better it would hold stones in its crop, which helped to break down tough foods. With no known predators on the island to fear, the dodo had no need to evolve its wings for flight, so despite not being particularly tasty, it easily fell prey to the early settlers. Animals introduced by settlers further threatened the dodo population by eating their eggs, and within a few years it had been driven to extinction.

In 1865, a British naturalist discovered a complete set of bones near Plaisance, and a stuffed exhibit is now on show in the Natural History Museum of the Mauritius Institute in Port Louis.

A multiplicity of life forms exists in the clear waters of Mauritius. Gardens of colourful **corals** thrive in the shallow, warm waters surrounding the island, and within the protective reefs live giant clams, primitive sponges and anemones, and gorgonias swaying in the current, colourful fish of all shapes and sizes as well as other curious creatures such as octopuses, giant eels, urchins and starfish. Damage to corals by boats, souvenir seekers and dredgers is a serious problem, however; the reefs are home to a vast range of other living creatures and once damaged, they are slow to recover – it takes a year for coral to grow 1cm (⅜in).

Conserving Mauritius' Natural Heritage

Just north of Port Louis, at Pamplemousses, lies the **Sir Seewoosagur Ramgoolam Botanic Garden**. Established in 1735, the gardens form the repository of the island's botanical heritage and are well known by naturalists around the world. Their large collection of both indigenous and exotic plants includes numerous species of palm, fruit and spice trees, pandanus, mahogany and ebony trees, while among other animals there are some resident tortoises, brought last century from Seychelles as they were in danger of extinction there.

The **Government Aviary** at **Rivière Noire** in the west of the island forms part of a sponsored scientific project which aims to encourage the breeding of rare bird species in danger of extinction. These species include the pink pigeon, echo parakeet and Mauritius kestrel. In 1973 a breeding programme, aimed at increasing the numbers of Mauritius kestrel and supported by the Mauritius Wildlife Appeal Fund, began operating – only just in time, as it was soon discovered that their numbers were down to single figures. After initial failures, the programme eventually resulted in the release of more than 300 into the wild. A similar captive breeding programme, aimed at increasing the number of pink pigeons from a low of 20, was started in 1976 and has now met with some success, while another breeding programme has been rescuing from the brink of extinction the world's rarest parakeet, the echo parakeet, of which there were a mere 15 in the wild in 1991.

The **Mauritius Marine Conservation Society** was formed in 1980 to promote an appreciation of marine life and an awareness of the need in Mauritius for this area of conservation. It seeks to create underwater parks to regenerate marine life and induce the government to enforce existing laws which control dynamite fishing, spear-fishing, net fishing, shell and coral collection, aquatic pollution and the general destruction of the reefs.

PLACES FOR BIRD-LOVERS TO VISIT

- The **Government Aviary** at Rivière Noire. Tours only by arrangement through selected tour operators.
- The **Casela Bird Park**, on the west of the island in the Black River district, featuring 2500 birds of 142 different species, as well as tigers and monkeys.
- **Le Domaine du Chasseur** near Mahébourg to see Mauritius kestrels being fed by hand.
- The **Mauritius Institute** in Port Louis to see a stuffed specimen of the dodo.

Opposite left: *The endemic Mauritius kestrel, recently saved from extinction.*
Opposite right: *A stuffed dodo in the Mauritius Institute, Port Louis.*
Below: *The reef provides a protective environment for all kinds of colourful fish.*

Right: *Some of the delicate artistry of the many coral forms found around Mauritius.*
Below: *The unspoilt beauty of the Black River Gorges National Park.*
Opposite top: A *classic schooner from the days of sail.*
Opposite bottom: *An old French map showing the island in 1753.*

FASCINATING FACTS ABOUT CORAL

Coral colonies are made up of tiny, sedentary creatures called polyps, which secrete limestone to form a skeleton. It is these organisms which give corals their brilliant colours; when they are closed, the coral becomes white or stone-coloured.

Corals reproduce once a year, in a mass spawning which occurs all over the reef during a single night. Like a slow, silent fireworks display, bundles of eggs and sperm are released and float to the surface, where they break up; the sperm seek eggs of the same species before all are dispersed by the tide. The fertilized eggs develop into planulae within a few days and sink to the bottom to take up residence as members of the new coral colony.

The age of some corals can be determined by 'reading' the dark and light bands of the skeleton, as one would date a tree by the rings of its trunk. Some living corals are hundreds of years old.

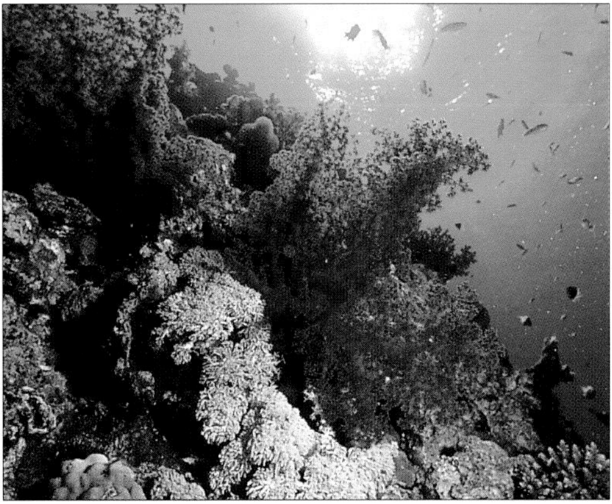

The government has declared a number of offshore islands as nature reserves in a bid to preserve indigenous fauna and flora. Likewise, certain inland areas have become nature reserves, such as the Macchabée-Bel Ombre Forest in the mountainous southwest of the island. Much of the Black River Gorges, Bel Ombre and Bassin Blanc area within this region was declared the country's first national park in 1994. Some mountain areas are under government control and permission must be obtained from the Conservator of Forests (tel: 675-4966) before they can be visited.

HISTORY IN BRIEF

Mauritius was left untouched as a Garden of Eden for aeons. The first recorded discovery of the island was made by Arab seamen who landed there in AD975. Although they gave it a name, Dinarobin ('silver island'), they left no evidence of their presence, and the island was allowed to slumber on peacefully until 1507 when the Portuguese sailor Domingo Fernandez came across it. The island was renamed Ilha do Cerne ('island of the swan'); the more romantic say that this was in honour of the ungainly land swan, the dodo, while others say the name was inspired by that of Fernandez's boat, *The Swan*. Despite the island's strategic position on the important shipping route to the East Indies, and despite introducing pigs, goats and oxen as food supplies, the Portuguese did not claim possession of Mauritius, and it was used for many years as a base by pirates.

The Dutch Presence

Just before the turn of the century, in 1598, the Dutch **Admiral van Warwyck** stopped on the southeast coast of Mauritius en route to the spice and silk markets of the East, and named the island after **Prince Maurice** (Maurits) of Nassau. During the next 40 years the island was visited periodically by the Dutch (one trip in 1606 brought with it the banana tree). Eventually they appointed a commanding officer who reached the island in 1638 and attempted to colonize it in order to exploit more systematically its luxuriant forests of ebony, a resource much prized in Europe. A hundred slaves were imported from Madagascar, and together with prisoners brought in from the East Indies as labourers, the population grew to over 500 from an original nucleus of 25. To improve their food supplies, the settlers brought Java deer, sheep, geese, ducks, pigeons and other animals, while another memorable

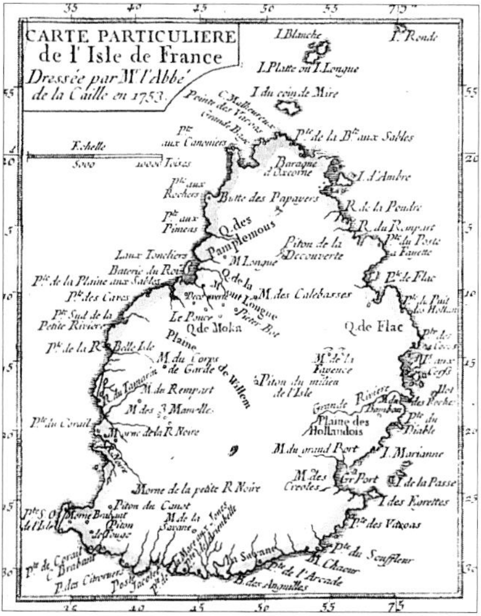

legacy of their stay on the island at this time was the introduction of sugar cane. Obstacles faced by the Dutch in their attempt at colonization included runaway slaves bent on retribution, pirates, cyclones, drought, disease and meagre resources. Not surprisingly, these problems proved to be the downfall of the Dutch settlers, who abandoned Mauritius in 1658 in favour of the station that had been established at the Cape of Good Hope in 1652.

By 1664, the Dutch had come to appreciate the value of Mauritius in the context of the sea route to the East Indies and decided to recolonize. Over the next few years they established a tannery and started building a road network. Less than half a century later, however, in 1710, the same obstacles that had caused them to abandon the island the first time round set the seal on their departure for a second and final time.

FOUNDING FATHER

Bertrand François Mahé de Labourdonnais (1699-1753), as governor and administrator of the Ile de France, was responsible for transforming this wild tropical island into a flourishing colony. In addition to all his efforts at improving the small colony, Labourdonnais also led a team to fight against the British in India, where he relieved the French territory of Pondicherry and captured Madras from the British. Despite his successes in both spheres, however, he was imprisoned in the Bastille for two years after falling out with the French governor of Pondicherry. Although eventually his name was cleared and he was released from prison, he died a broken man at the age of 54.

The French Influence

Only five years passed before the French landed on the island in 1715 and named it Ile de France, although it was not until 1721 that they actually occupied the island. For 14 years thereafter, not much progress was achieved; the turning point came in 1735, when **Bertrand François Mahé de Labourdonnais**, known afterwards as the 'father of the island', was made governor. This man of vision and energy restored law and order to the island and expanded and developed Port Louis into a viable port and capital. To Labourdonnais goes the credit for the introduction of wheat and

Right: *Bertrand François Mahé de Labourdonnais, dynamic French governor of Mauritius during the 18th century.*

Opposite: *An impressive colonial plantation house, set among the sugar estates in the north of the island.*

cotton and the large-scale planting of sugar cane, the construction of roads and fortifications, Government House, a hospital and houses and, in conjunction with the establishment of Port Louis as a port, the creation of a ship-building industry.

Within half a century the island's population was well established with some 60,000 inhabitants, and during this time the colony's fortunes rose and fell under the leadership of the Intendant, **Pierre Poivre**, and the governor, **François, Vicomte de Souillac** respectively. Then in 1790, a mini-revolution took place on Mauritius, echoing events that had taken place in France the previous year, and there followed 13 years of self-rule, which lasted until Napoleon sent out a governor to restore law and order in the colony.

During this period Mauritius experienced what could be termed the 'golden age of piracy'. Pirates and corsairs under French protection used the island as a base for mercilessly plundering the British vessels which travelled along the shipping route to the East Indies. In 1802, the British retaliated by blockading the island. Coming after a century of antagonism between British and French, the attack was not motivated solely by this piracy, however – the British also wished to undermine the strategic position of the French in the Indian Ocean in order to safeguard their important colony of India. In August 1810 a fierce battle, the **Battle of Grand Port**, was fought in the bay of the same name in the southeast of the island – the only naval battle to be won by France during the reign of Napoleon. The British retired hurt, but just before the end of that year they launched a successful surprise attack on the north of the island from Cap Malheureux. The neighbouring island of Réunion was conquered the same year.

The Golden Age of Pirates

Throughout the 18th century, ships sailing between Africa and the Far East regularly fell victim to **pirates**. So well established were these highwaymen of the seas that they reputedly formed a pirates' republic, **Libertalia**, in Madagascar in 1685. With the decline of Mauritius in the mid-18th century under the French East India Company, the pirate colony migrated here; the French began to support the pirates to safeguard their own vessels and prey on British ships, and Port Louis became notorious as a haven for corsairs and a thriving marketplace for pirate booty.

The Frenchman **Robert Surcouf** came to be known as the 'king of the Corsairs', and the British offered a reward of 250,000 francs for him, dead or alive. However, the prosperity generated on the island by pirate activity was appreciated by the local business community, which helped to finance him; as a personal friend of Napoleon, he also received the support of the French government.

Above: *The monument commemorating the Battle of Grand Port in 1810.*

Philately

Mauritius is well known among philatelists as one of the first countries in the world to have released a postage stamp – now one of the rarest. Five hundred stamps of the first issue with a value of 1d and 2d were used by Lady Gomm, wife of the governor, to post invitations to a ball at the governor's residence, Le Réduit, in 1847. Instead of the words 'Post Paid', 'Post Office' was mistakenly printed on the stamps. A One-Penny Red and a Two-Penny Blue were recently acquired by a group of Mauritian businessmen at an auction in Geneva, and are exhibited at the Blue Penny Museum (tel: 210-8176, fax: 210-9243) at Le Caudan Waterfront in Port Louis.

British Rule

The first British governor was **Robert Farquhar**, who very generously offered the French inhabitants capitulation terms that allowed them to preserve their French laws, customs, language, religion and property; this was formalized in the Treaty of Paris of 1814, whereby the British returned the island of Réunion to France but retained Mauritius, Rodrigues and Seychelles. At the same time the British gave the island its old Dutch name of Mauritius.

Mauritius enjoyed over a century and a half of reasonably peaceful British rule; French culture continued to dominate, however, and has endured to the present day, notably in the form of the French language which is spoken by most people. Under Farquhar, the country's economy developed into one based on agriculture (especially the production of sugar), roads were built, and Port Louis became a free trading centre.

Despite the formal abolition of **slavery** in 1833 in other parts of the British Empire, plantation owners in Mauritius defied the ruling and continued to practise slavery until 1835. This proved to be a turning point in the island's history, as the ending of slavery led to the mass immigration from the Indian subcontinent of some 200,000 Hindu and Moslem indentured labourers. Lured

HISTORICAL CALENDAR

AD975 Arabs land on the island and name it Dinarobin.
1511 Portuguese explorers arrive, name the island Ilha do Cirne ('isle of the swan').
1598 Dutch traders stop en route to the East Indies, and name the island Mauritius.
1638 The Dutch attempt to colonize Mauritius.
1658 They abandon the colony for the Cape of Good Hope.
1664 Recolonization by the Dutch.
1710 The Dutch leave the island permanently.
1715 The French arrive in Mauritius, naming the island Ile de France.
1721 Ile de France is occupied by the French.
1735 Labourdonnais begins to transform the island.
1790 Revolution takes place, links with France cut, Mauritius becomes a pirate retreat.
1802 Port Louis blockaded by British sailors in protest against piracy. The battle of Grand Port is won by the French. The British take the island in a surprise attack in December.
1814 Mauritius is ceded to the British by the Treaty of Paris.
1835 The abolition of slavery sees the start of a massive influx of Indian labour.
1959 Universal franchise is granted.
1968 Mauritius wins independence from Britain.
1992 Republic is declared.

by the promise of a better life, they came to work on the sugar-cane plantations in conditions which were initially not much better than slavery. By 1909 immigration had ceased, but the large Indian population was there to stay and rapidly became the majority group, staking its claim in Mauritius when universal franchise was granted in 1959.

Although **independence** was won from Britain in 1968, the island remained part of the British Commonwealth with the Queen as its head, represented by a governor general. The first prime minister, Sir Seewoosagur Ramgoolam, was of Hindu origin. Highly regarded by many Mauritians, he held office until 1982, when another Hindu Mauritian, Anerood Jugnauth, became prime minister. Mauritius proclaimed itself a republic on 12 March 1992, with Veerasamy Ringadoo as the first president. Jugnauth is currently president.

GOVERNMENT AND ECONOMY

The parliamentary system of Mauritius owes much to the British Westminster system; here, the president is the ceremonial head of state, while executive power is held by the cabinet, headed by a prime minister who is the leader of the majority group in parliament. According to the constitution, general elections must be held every five years. Each of the 20 constituencies in Mauritius returns

LEADING LIGHT

Although he trained and qualified as a doctor in England, **Sir Seewoosagur Ramgoolam** (1900-1985) had a long and illustrious political career in Mauritius. With a reputation as a speaker with moderate views, he became a member of the Labour party in 1948, and in 1965 led the Labour Party delegation to the Constitutional Conference in London, when independence was agreed. Three years later he became the country's first Prime Minister. In 1982 he suffered his only political defeat, when the MMM won the general election and Anerood Jugnauth became Prime Minister; Ramgoolam was appointed Governor General. A leading and well-respected figure on the island for many decades, his name has been given to the airport, the botanic gardens at Pamplemousses, and a number of public buildings, streets and other places on the island.

SUGAR

The sugar industry, having been such an important part of the island's economy for so long, has evolved into a highly sophisticated industry. Crystallized sugar is certainly not the only product derived from the sugar cane plant: the residual liquid left over from the crystallizing process is sold as molasses, used in cattle feed and in rum, the scum on the top of the liquid is used as fertilizer, and the vegetable remains of the cane, left after the juice has been extracted, is used as fuel, not only for running the sugar factories, but also as part of the island's general electricity supply.

three members and Rodrigues two, while up to eight 'best losers' can be appointed for ethnic balance in the House. Due to the 'first past the post' principle, candidates can be elected with less than 50% of the votes. However, with strong bipolarization, small parties cannot hope to see their candidates elected and this leads to political alliances – government by coalition is a standard feature of Mauritian politics. The 1991 election was won jointly by the MSM (Mouvement Socialist Militant), the MMM (Mouvement Militant Mauricien) and the MTD (Mouvement Travaillist Démocratique). After a split within the MMM, this party left the government while some of its leading members chose to create a new party, the RMM (Rassemblement Militant Mauricien). The last election, in December 1995, was won by the coalition of the PTr (Parti Travailliste, or Labour Party) with the MMM. However, in June 1998, a new crisis lead the MMM to quit the government. At this stage, with the PTr ruling alone, the MMM has again joined forces with the MSM. They represent the main opposition block. Cassam Uteem is currently president.

The Mauritian legal system is based on both French and English law. The constitution guarantees the independence of the Judiciary. The island is divided into nine administrative districts, and Rodrigues forms the tenth.

Below: *Sugar piling up inside a Port Louis factory.*
Opposite: *Cane fields cover vast reaches of the Mauritian countryside.*

Economy

Thanks to the Dutch who introduced its cultivation in 1639, **sugar** was the mainstay of the Mauritian economy for years. Originally grown to provide alcohol for the making of 'arrack', a crude drink popular with sailors, sugar cane was later propagated widely as it was judged the crop best able to withstand the ravages of the occasional cyclones.

Around 80% of the island's arable land was once planted with sugar, and the island's fortunes rose and fell with those of the sugar industry. By 1985 this proportion had dropped considerably – testimony to the growing dominance of the Export Processing Zone (EPZ) economic structure, a concept which was introduced in the 1970s. Its precursor of the previous decade, the policy of Import Substitution Industrialization (ISI), encouraged the production of foodstuffs and soft drinks, cement, paint and plastics (to name a few) to the extent that Mauritius could export them to other islands in the area. In addition to the ISI and the more far-reaching EPZ, which has encouraged foreign investment, the island has recently been promoted as an **offshore banking centre**; a national **stock exchange** was established in 1989 and since 1992 legislation has been amended to transform Port Louis' harbour area into a 'free port'. Furthermore, **tourism** has taken off as a strong industry in its own right in recent years. Combining these factors, Mauritius' economy has gone from strength to strength, unemployment is negligible, and the country has rapidly progressed from being a Third World backwater to an important economic entity in the region within only a few decades.

FOREIGN INVESTMENT

Foreign investors can take advantage of generous financial incentives such as exemption from tax and customs duties, as well as the freedom to repatriate capital and dividends. Further investment incentives include relatively cheap trained labour and a stable political environment.

The Export Processing Zone

As the sugar boom of the 1970s lost its sparkle and the ISI plan reached its limits, the **Export Processing Zone** concept started gaining ground, just in time to create some diversity in an economy that was far too dependent on only one crop. Established in 1970 as much to absorb a burgeoning labour force as to attract foreign investment, the EPZ succeeded in rapidly reducing unemployment from a high of 25% in 1983 to full employment in 1990; since then the country has had to import foreign workers, with some 10,000 coming into the country in 1994. Today the EPZ accounts for over 65% of Mauritian exports through more than 560 enterprises. **Textile** firms dominate EPZ activity these days, resulting somewhat ironically in tropical Mauritius becoming one of the largest exporters of knitwear in the world, and in textiles overtaking sugar as the island's primary export. Although most of the goods are aimed at the export market, many are also available in Mauritius. Efforts are now being made to diversify the EPZ base further with manufacturers of a wide range of commercial goods being encouraged to set up business on the island.

Tourism

The third largest employer and supplier of foreign exchange is tourism, which has, however, proved to be a double-edged sword. In its infancy during the 1950s, tourism only took off towards the end of the 1970s and became well established during the economic upswing of the early 1980s. However, the government recognized the dangers of overdeveloping the tourism industry and put a halt to further hotel development in 1990. At present there are over 100 hotels offering close on 6000 beds, as well as many smaller guesthouses and self-catering establishments.

The Dawn of Tourism

For Mauritius' first tourists, conditions were a far cry from what they are today. Michael Malim, in his book, *Island of the Swan* (1952), describes the 'hotel' he is faced with after receiving the disheartening warning, 'We don't exactly cater for tourists':

'On the face of it there was little to suggest that anyone had lived there for years. The place was simply a large, wooden barn perched on a stone platform about five feet high. It was more or less white, though much of the paint had flaked away. A tin canopy, supported by rusty iron stanchions rising from an iron balustrade, sheltered the verandah which ran the whole width of the building. In places it was sagging away from the *façade*. There was an appalling sense of despair about the whole contraption... It seemed to long to slither from its platform into the jungle of weeds and shrubs about it, and disintegrate there into a heap of mouldering timber.'

Left: *The highly rated Royal Palm Hotel.*
Opposite: *The drama of fishing on the reef, with fishermen poling their wooden boats around another generous catch.*

Although large numbers of visitors place heavy demands on the island's resources, tourist arrivals in 1994 amounted to 400,000 people. To keep Mauritius as an exclusive rather than a backpacker destination, charter flights are not permitted. The largest number of tourists each year comes from Réunion, followed by France, South Africa, Germany, the United Kingdom and Australia.

RAILWAY WALK

A train service ran in Mauritius for almost 100 years. One line connected Port Louis with the plateau towns and Mahébourg in the southeast, then headed round to Souillac on the south coast, and another traversed the northern sugar fields and ran down the east coast to Grande Rivière Sud-Est.

Although the service as such ended in 1964, the railway lines and bridges remain intact in several places, making excellent routes for walks in the countryside.

Agriculture

Back in the days when Mauritius exported only agricultural products, **tea** was its second currency earner after sugar. Still grown in the highlands around Curepipe, tea is strongly subsidized for social and political reasons. It lacks a strong flavour, however, and is used in blends with the more flavoursome teas grown in other countries at the higher altitudes necessary for such flavour. Some tea sold locally is flavoured with vanilla pods, lending it a distinctive perfumed taste.

Cultivation of **tobacco**, which at one time was Mauritius' third most important crop, has not shown much promise as a developing economic activity; on the other hand, **flowers**, especially anthuriums, as well as **tropical fruits** such as pineapples, mangoes and litchis, are now being exported, and their contribution to the country's foreign trade is expected to increase significantly by the end of the century.

The **fishing** industry is divided between small-scale fishermen and commercial fishing enterprises. Problems of supply arose from inshore fishing areas being over-exploited, and at one stage in the early 1980s Mauritius was importing the bulk of its fish; efforts are now being made to develop commercial fishing ventures offshore. Although the island is self-sufficient in poultry and pork, and there is some cattle production on local estates, most **meat** has to be imported.

Right: *A view from the sea of Port Louis harbour.*

TAXI-TRAINS

Taxi-trains or share-taxis are a form of public transport characteristic to Mauritius, and occupy the gaps in the market left by taxis and buses. Basically communal taxis, these operate on more or less standard routes (with a few detours), especially where buses are not very frequent. The fares, split among the passengers, are comparable to bus fares. To catch a taxi-train, simply flag down a regular taxi and find out whether it is for private or communal use.

Infrastructure

Although fairly extensive, the **road network** in Mauritius is generally confusing to most visitors. Originally built to provide access to the cane fields, the road grid's seemingly haphazard design makes it fairly easy to get lost. Mauritius has long been notorious for its potholed roads, but relatively recently the government made a concerted effort to resurface roads across the island. In built-up areas, the lack of a pavement creates further dangers. In the last decade the island's only highway has been extended to Grand Baie, making access between north and south quicker and easier: it runs from Plaisance in the southeast through the centre of the island to Port Louis in the northwest and Grand Baie in the north. Land transport is now solely by road, as the **railway system**, which joined the north and the south of the island for nearly a century, stopped operating in 1964.

The main **harbour**, at Port Louis, is a natural harbour which has been enlarged to include five deep-water quays, two fishing quays and three lighterage quays. It includes a container terminal as well as terminals for handling bulk sugar, oil, wheat and cement. The government is in the process of establishing Port Louis as a 'free port' as part of a strategy to develop the island as a regional trade centre in the Indian Ocean.

Air Mauritius, the national carrier, operates a fleet of Boeing 747s, Airbus A340-300s, Boeing 767 ERs, ATR 42s and Bell Jet Ranger helicopters – two of each craft. Its air network extends to Europe, India, the Far East and various cities in southern Africa.

THE PEOPLE

Because of the limited size of the island, the population explosion on Mauritius has been keenly felt. In the space of 160 years the population has grown from 100,000 to 1,100,000; this has resulted in extremely high population density and, at one stage, widespread unemployment. The true impact of unemployment was promptly halted in the late 1980s when the Export Processing Zone concept finally became well established, leading to mass employment opportunities.

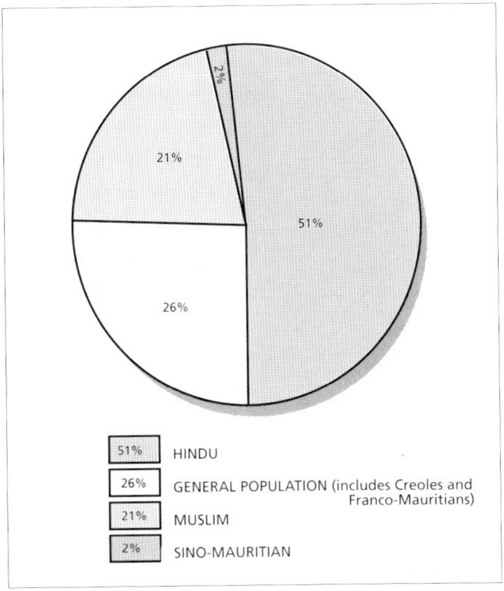

POPULATION ANALYSIS

The uneven concentration of people in the centre of the island could give one the impression, when driving around the coastal plains, that the vast tracts of agricultural land imply low population density. Many parts are isolated, with few pedestrians on the roads. But with a population density estimated at 576 people per square kilometre (1492 per square mile), Mauritius is actually the third most densely populated place in the world.

The migration of the population to the central plateau started in the early 1860s when people fled to the uplands to escape a malaria epidemic in Port Louis. A second wave of migration took place only a few years later, when people sought to escape the coastal ravages of cyclones as well as malaria and cholera epidemics; the opening of the railway at the same time also contributed to the rapid urbanization of the interior in the 1860s. Today, the cooler temperatures of the interior are a major attraction for permanent residents, and while over 140,000 people live in the capital and commercial centre of Port Louis, some 30% of the population lives in Curepipe and the other dormitory towns of the central plateau.

Traditional Cultures

Mauritius is a veritable melting pot embracing a diversity of cultures, something on which its people pride themselves. The largest cultural group is made up of people with **Indian** roots, and broadly speaking, comprises Hindus originating from northern India (the largest ethnic grouping), Tamils from southern India, and Muslims from western India (who form the smallest part of the group).

Top left: *A Hindu woman, her traditional finery complemented by a garland of frangipani flowers.*
Top right: *Rodriguan boys stop for an ice-cream on a hot summer's day.*
Above: *This cheerful Creole woman epitomizes the colour and vibrancy of the tropical island.*

While the Indians arrived after the ending of slavery in 1835 to work on the sugar plantations, the **Creoles** owe part of their ancestry to the first slaves who were imported from Madagascar and possibly the east coast of Africa. The arrival of the **Chinese**, mostly from Canton, dates from after 1826. Most Europeans are of French descent and stem from the settlers who arrived during the colonization of the island by France. **Franco-Mauritians** have remained prominent in the sugar industry and are still the largest landowners. Some have successfully invested dividends from this agricultural capital in the industrial sector, while for others, their fortunes are on the decline as a result of their dwindling numbers and thus their fading influence. Middle-class Indo-Mauritians work mostly in the civil service, though today the best trained among them are employed in the private sector. The community of Chinese origin is a very dynamic minority, with a high percentage of trained professionals. Owners of small retail shops 50 years ago, the Sino-Mauritians have taken a prominent place in the main sectors of economic life today.

Language

English is the official language, but while it is a compulsory subject at school and is the language of government and business, not everybody feels comfortable speaking it. **French** is more widely spoken and is dominant in the media, although it is mother tongue to only a small proportion of the population.

The language spoken most by Mauritians, however, is **Creole** (or Kreol). Originating as the common tongue among slaves of differing origins, and between them and the colonists, the lingua franca of the island is based largely on French with elements of English, Hindi, Chinese and Malagasy. It is a picturesque language, humorous and very pliable, and unstandardized in grammar and spelling alike. Despite its widespread use, however, it is neither taught in school nor recognized officially.

Language Tips

English	Creole
Hello	Bonzour
How are you?	Koman ou ete?
Fine thanks	Mon byen, mersi
Goodbye	Orewar
Please	Silvouple
Thank you	Mersi
How much is this?	Kombyen i ete
I don't understand	Mo pas comprend
No problem	Pena problème
Alright	Correc
Not alright	Pas correc
Do you have...?	Ou ena...?

Bhojpuri, a language from northern India which is linked to Hindi, is spoken by many Indo-Mauritians. With generations of French influence it has diverged from the Bhojpuri spoken in India, and lacking prestige, it appears to be on the wane, losing popularity to Creole. **Hindi** itself is used for official purposes, such as broadcasts, but it is not widely spoken as a home language. To a lesser extent, various other Indian languages are in use, as well as **Hakka**, **Mandarin** and **Cantonese**.

Education

Schooling is free and while not compulsory, 90% of children attend school; the literacy rate, at over 95%, is one of the highest in the world. Further practical training is provided by various organizations, and the annual intake of the **University of Mauritius** is always on the rise.

Right: *The symmetrical flourishes of one of Port Louis' colourful Chinese pagodas, which is located on the edge of the city.*

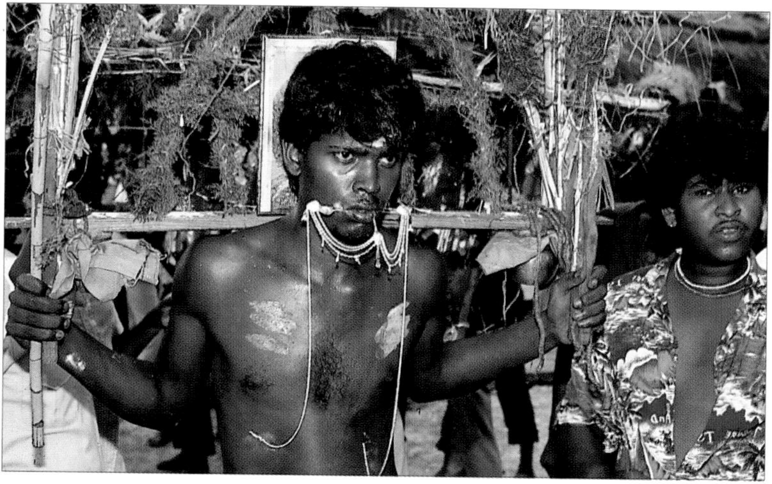

Above: *A Tamil Hindu pilgrim, his skin and mouth pierced with needles, carries a* cavadee *as part of the celebration of the same name, held in late January or early February.*
Opposite: *These wooden structures, decked in bright flowers, are a central part of the Cavadee procession.*

Religion

With 87 denominations on the island, religion plays a major part in the island's cultural activities. Numerous churches, mosques, pagodas and temples exist, sometimes within very close proximity of each other, bearing testimony to the remarkable level of religious and cultural tolerance. The largest religious grouping is made up of **Hindus**, who account for 51% of the population, followed by **Christians** (mainly Roman Catholics) at 25%. Thereafter, **Islam** is the next most popular religion, practised by 21% of Mauritians, and **Buddhism** the fourth.

Mauritians enjoy complete freedom of worship, and their faiths are expressed in the many festivals held each year. Accommodating the holy days of the various religions, Mauritius once enjoyed the dubious distinction of having the most public holidays in the world! These days, however, the public holiday list has been trimmed from a generous 30 to a more viable 13. With the large number of festivals, visitors may well be lucky enough to witness the celebrations of one of the faiths.

Tamil Hindus practise the exotic rituals of fire-walking, sword-climbing and tongue-piercing on certain festival days. Mauritian Muslims are largely Sunnis but the Shiite practice of body chastisement during the Ghoons festival remains.

Cavadee, one of the most spectacular of the Hindu festivals, takes place in January or February and is preceded by 10 days of prayers and fasting. A wooden arch or *cavadee*, decorated with flowers and with pots of milk hanging from each end, is carried to the temple. Beforehand, penitents insert skewers and hooks into their cheeks, tongue, chest and back. The more devout, in a state of trance, are even able to pull a cart attached to these hooks.

Just as incredible to the Western eye is the Hindu ritual of fire-walking, also known as **Teemeedee**, which takes place at Tamil temples in the late afternoons between October and March. Devotees, dressed in yellow and pink, use the ritual as a means of asking for pardon and offering thanks for favours. A bed of hot coals is prepared and a goat's neck is slit so that its blood can be poured around the coals to keep out bad spirits. Only those who are scrupulously clean both inside and out can take part; the worshipper must therefore fast, pray and meditate for at least 10 days beforehand and take a ritual bath just prior to the act. Some mothers carry their babies across, and even children participate in the ritual, encouraged by the chanting of supporters, the sound of trumpets and beating of drums as well as the heady odour of incense and camphor. As participants leave the embers, they dip their feet into a basin of milk.

Other Hindu festivals include **Diwali**, the festival of lights, which celebrates the triumph of good over evil with lights and fire-crackers, the sharing of cakes with friends, and the offering of fruit, sweets and flowers to Laksmi, goddess of wealth; **Maha Shivaratree**, one of the biggest festivals on the Hindu calendar, which involves a pilgrimage to Grand Bassin for ritual cleansing (its waters are said to be connected to those of the sacred Ganges River in India); and **Holi**, feast of fire and colour, at

SPIRITS AND SORCERY

Once used to describe a charm or talisman, the term ***gris-gris*** has become more vague and generalized to denote magic and witchcraft in varying forms, and people's belief in spirits. Brought across to Mauritius by the early African slaves, *gris-gris* was outlawed by the European settlers, and remains illegal. Despite this, it still has some influence on the behaviour and religious practices of the Creoles on the island, and **witchdoctors** or *longanists* continue to lead a covert existence, consulted in the hopes that they can solve all sorts of problems. Memories of it linger on in the names of the village of Gris Gris on the south coast and Ville Noire ('black town') near Mahébourg.

PERE LAVAL

After qualifying in France as a doctor, **Père Laval** became a missionary in Mauritius in 1841, at the age of 38. Over the next 23 years, his work with the poor and outcast, slaves and lepers was much appreciated by thousands of Mauritians. He was, however, resented by some in the ruling classes, although his countless good deeds and his missionary work were finally recognized by his beatification by Pope John Paul in 1979.

Above: *A dragon costume is fitted in preparation for the Chinese New Year festivities – to the amusement of the onlookers!*

which an effigy of the wicked Holika is burnt to symbolize the triumph over evil. The latter is also celebrated with fountains of coloured water (tourists who get too close will get wet!). In India, **Gangan Asnan** involves immersion in the Ganges for purification; in Mauritius, Hindus go down to the sea or to Ganga Talao (Grand Bassin) for an equivalent ceremony.

As well as the usual holy days, Mauritian Christians celebrate the festival of **Père Laval** on 9 September. On the anniversary of this saint's death, thousands of Mauritians and even people from further afield converge on Sainte Croix, Port Louis, to pray at his tomb. Masses are held continuously from 16:00 the day before until midday. On **All Souls' Day** Christians flock to cemeteries to place flowers on the graves, and prayers are said for the salvation of the dead. The ritual washing of graves demonstrates African influences.

Eid-ul-Fitr marks the end of the fast of **Ramadan** for the Moslems, who also celebrate **Ghoons**, a festival commemorating the martyrdom of Mohammed's nephew, Imam Hussein. It bears some similarity in form to the Hindu Cavadee; a decorated bamboo structure or *ghoon* is carried through the streets of Port Louis while participants, their cheeks, tongue and skin pierced with needles, inflict various forms of torture on themselves in repentance. However, Ghoons is no longer widely celebrated.

Visitors to Mauritius may also be interested to see the colourful **Chinese New Year** or **Spring Festival** celebrations. Homes are decked out in red, firecrackers are let off to drive away evil spirits, and special foods are prepared. The Dragon Dance is a highlight, performed at sunset by eight or more people wearing a dragon costume with a colourful and ornately decorated mask.

The tourist office can supply interested visitors with the dates on which religious rituals and festivals are to take place, as many of them vary from year to year.

The Séga

The obsessive beat of the séga has its roots in Africa, and no doubt the dance was brought across to Mauritius (and other Indian Ocean islands) by the slaves. Historical records indicate that this erotically suggestive **Creole dance** was evolved as a means of bemoaning hard working conditions; slaves met on the beach at night around a fire, where supplies of rum assisted their emotional outpourings. The tone and direction of the séga was determined by the beating of a goatskin drum called a **'ravanne'** accompanied by a small triangle and a container of dried peas or small stones, the **'maravanne'**.

Dressed in vividly coloured skirts, the women weave flirtatiously in front of the men with much swaying of hips. A solo **singer** supplies the story (usually in Creole) while a chorus echoes the refrain. The tempo slowly increases and, with the dancing becoming more and more provocative, the mood is transformed from one of gentle melancholy to a frenzy of passion, before eventually dying down again. The players traditionally perform in front of an eager audience who encourage them with the clapping of hands and the stamping of feet and by joining in with the chorus.

In response to tourist demand, the séga has become more and more commercialized over the last couple of decades; some say that today it is a far cry from the original dance form. Many hotels organize a weekly show

Festivals and Holidays

Nov-Mar	Hindu (Tamil)	Fire-walking
1/2 Jan*		New Year
Jan	Moslem	Yaum un Nabi
Jan/Feb*	Hindu (Tamil)	Cavadee
Jan/Feb*	Chinese	Spring Festival/ New Year
Feb/Mar*	Hindu	Maha Shivaratree
Feb/Mar	Hindu	Holi
12 Mar*		Independence Day
Mar/Apr*	Telegu	Ougadi
Mar/Apr	Christian	Easter
1 May*		Labour Day
Aug/Sept*	Hindu (Marathi)	Ganesh Chaturthi
9 Sept	Christian	Père Laval
Oct/Nov*	Hindu	Diwali
1 Nov*	Christian	All Saints' Day
	Hindu	Ganga Asnan
25 Dec*	Christian	Christmas Day

Moslems celebrate Eid-ul-Fitr and Eid-ul-Adha according to the Islamic calendar, subject to the phases of the moon.
** public holidays*

Below: *A display of séga dancing taking place in one of the island's hotels.*

Dive Sights

The more experienced diver can tailor a diving holiday to take in shelf dives, wreck dives, night dives and diving trips to nearby islands.

Some of the exotic fish divers come across are parrotfish, thick-lipped groupers, wrasses, sweetlips, angelfish and squirrelfish, boxfish, trumpet fish and clown fish. Colourful sponges, corals, sea anemones and fan worms adorn the marine underworld. Divers may take the opportunity to explore numerous wrecks from the 18th and 19th centuries, as well as those that have been deliberately sunk in recent times to create artificial reefs.

for their guests which can prove to be highly enjoyable as they are invited onto the dance floor by the travelling séga troupe to learn the simple steps. Under the light of the moon with the waves gently lapping at the nearby shore, the beat of the séga is marvellously evocative.

Sport and Recreation

As a warm, year-round destination with calm, turquoise, coral-belted lagoons, Mauritius is certainly a **water sport** playground. Scuba diving, snorkelling, windsurfing, sailing and big-game fishing are among the wide range of activities catered for on the island, many of them by the big hotels as well as by independent organizations. Out of the water, Mauritians are particularly fond of **soccer**, and basketball and volleyball are growing in popularity. Although jockeys are mainly South African, **horse-racing** draws huge crowds to the Champ de Mars in Port Louis during the winter months.

No matter their level of proficiency, locals and holiday-makers alike enjoy **diving** and **snorkelling** in the veritable fairyland of coral gardens found along many parts of the coast. With surface water temperatures outside the reef ranging from 22°C (72°F) in August and September to 27°C (81°F) in March, and with higher summer temperatures in the lagoons within the reef, a wetsuit is not necessary for dives to a depth of 20m (66ft). Visibility near the reef is at its best in the winter, but for offshore dives, summer is a better time, as the warm waters attract an abundance of fish.

Most diving schools, whether independent or allied to hotels, are affiliated to the Mauritius Scuba Diving Association which sees to it that international diving standards are adhered to, in terms of both

Below: *Scuba diving on the reef in the company of a clown fish.*

Opposite: *Pleasure cruises, water-skiing and sailing are just some of the water sports available on Mauritius.*

Nasties of the Reef

Spines from certain types of **sea urchin** can be very hard to remove once embedded in your foot, and sometimes result in infection. If this does happen and you are not able to rely on hotel medical facilities, first see if you can tap the knowledge of a local fisherman to help you extract the spine correctly, otherwise you will need to see a doctor. In the shallows and near the reef, other dangers include the lethal **stonefish**, easy to tread on as it lies motionless on the sandy bottom with just its eyes showing. Wear old shoes in the water to avoid treading on urchins and stonefish, and don't touch any creature you are unsure of. Certain live **shells** of the cone family can inflict painful stings, some of which may be fatal if not treated promptly. The slow-moving red-and-white-striped **lion-fish** has poisonous fins and should be avoided. Happily, shark attacks are almost unheard of inside the lagoon, although sharks are found outside it.

instruction and the equipment supplied. Beginners can take their first diving lessons in some hotel swimming pools, progressing to shallow sea dives if they show ability within a few lessons. If you are qualified, remember to bring your diving certification as proof of your abilities.

Diving facilities are usually charged for by the hotels, in contrast with most other water sports, such as snorkelling. If you bring your own snorkelling gear, make sure you also bring protective footwear and gloves to guard against injury from sea urchins and a few other nasties. The use of spear guns is strictly prohibited, as is the removal of any live or dead coral or shells from the lagoon or reef. If diving and snorkelling don't appeal to you, many hotels have **glass-bottomed boats** which take guests out for a more leisurely examination of the reef.

Surfing is best at Tamarin Bay on the west coast, although according to locals, surf conditions have deteriorated in recent years.

Mauritius has earned itself a name for **big-game fishing** among anglers around the world, and indeed has held world records in several categories. The best fishing grounds lie off the west coast, where fish may be caught less than a kilometre (half a mile) offshore during the summer months. Fully equipped boats can be hired from the hotels, and if you wish, a professional taxidermist will mount your catch and later ship it to you anywhere in the world.

The centre of **sailing** activities is Grand Baie. Many hotels here and at other resorts on the island have small sailing craft such as Lasers available free of charge for use within the sheltered lagoon areas, and some will even provide free basic instruction in sailing. Others have catamarans available for use by their guests. Private yacht charter

Above: *Taking the plunge: divers preparing to explore the wonders of the reef. Most of the large hotels offer diving instruction and will arrange excursions.*

for day trips and excursions of several days is available through local travel agents; trips can be organized to offshore islands as well as to Réunion. The competitive sailing season is during July and August when the southeast trade winds are at their strongest; depending on demand, the Beachcomber Crossing from Mauritius to Durban, South Africa, takes place in August.

For a breath of fresh air, there are a number of excellent places for **walking**, **hiking** and **climbing**. The most interesting walk is to the top of Pieter Both mountain overlooking Port Louis, although it is more demanding than most and should be done with the help of a professional guide; rock-climbing is also possible here. Other walks, including le Pouce, la Montagne du Rempart, le Piton du Milieu, les Trois Mamelles, le Corps de Garde, le Morne and la Tourelle de Tamarin, are not so taxing and generally take about half a day. Plaine Champagne provides a cooler and potentially easier place to walk, while Yemen on the west coast is a good place for an easy ramble which doesn't involve negotiating mountains!

Most of the large hotels have good all-weather **tennis** courts, often with spotlights for use at night-time; equipment can be hired. There are a number of **golf** courses on Mauritius, mostly located at the big hotels. If you are not staying at a hotel with a golf course, you can still play after paying a small entry fee. If you intend to play much

When Planning a Walk

Equipment needed is usually only a pair of good walking shoes, raingear and a rucksack for water and food.

The walking and hiking club at Beau Bassin welcomes inquiries from visitors (see p. 121). Often, permission to climb mountains must first be obtained from the Conservator of Forests, Botanical Garden Street, Curepipe, (tel: 675-4966) as many of the mountains are government land. Occasionally permission must be obtained from private landowners whose land must be crossed before the mountain can be ascended.

golf, consider bringing your own clubs. The main international competition is held in April at le Morne, and there is now one in March at Belle Mare Plage.

There are two **horse-riding** clubs on Mauritius which provide jumping and dressage lessons. The Club Hippique de Maurice in Floréal allows temporary membership, while the Ecuries du Domaine, at Le Domaine les Pailles near Port Louis, can arrange lessons for groups of tourists and nature trails on horseback. In a less formal setting, various small stables near resorts at Belle Mare, Le Morne and Balaclava provide horses for tourists.

PETANQUE

Tourists may enjoy watching a game of **pétanque**, a French variation on bowls. A marker ball is thrown on a course without boundaries, following which the players attempt to get their ball nearest the jack. This gentle game, which requires no special skill except reasonable hand-eye coordination, is a popular amusement among Mauritians.

Hunting has been practised in Mauritius since deer were introduced from Java in 1639. A limit of 3000 is put on the number of deer which may be killed each year so that a population of 60,000 animals can be maintained. Deer-hunting takes place in reserves on the west and east coasts from June to September. At other times of the year wild boar, guinea fowl, quail, partridge and hare may be hunted. Local tour operators are able to organize day, overnight and weekend hunts. Le Domaine du Chasseur in the southeast is an area which has been especially reserved for hunting purposes; here one can hunt all year round.

Gambling has become a popular tourist attraction and several casinos exist around the island. These are to be found at Trou aux Biches in the north, and La Pirogue, the Berjaya Le Morne and Beachcomber Le Paradis in the west of the island. On the east coast the casinos are at Belle Mare Plage, Le Touessrok and Le St Géran. Curepipe has the Casino de Maurice. In Port Louis the Caudan Waterfront and Le Domaine Les Pailles each have a casino. The usual blackjack, roulette and one-armed bandits are offered by the coastal hotels. Exchange control permission is usually given by the government for the transfer of winnings by a nonresident. You may not take photographs inside casinos, and children under the age of 18 are not permitted entry.

Left: *A holiday in Mauritius provides a golden opportunity to try out all kinds of water sports in the relative safety of the lagoons.*

HEART OF PALM

An entire tree, which takes about four years to grow big enough, must be sacrificed to obtain its edible 'heart'. Palm plantations exist solely to satisfy the culinary demand for this delicacy which has existed since the Dutch occupation.

Only a third of the heart (weighing about 1.8kg; 4lbs) can be eaten. It must be quickly extracted from its protective fibrous sheath before the centre is cut out in a bath of milk and water: this way the ivory-coloured flesh is shielded from oxidation and discolouration is prevented. It is then cooked in the milk mixture. Its texture, once cooked, ranges from crisp to soft (but not limp). The taste is subtle and delicate and the heart should never be prepared with strong spices and condiments. It is often eaten as a salad, with seafood or in a soufflé.

Food and Drink

Mauritius is a delight for anyone who wishes to try a variety of culinary treats. Reflecting the country's diverse cultural heritage, Mauritian dishes are derived from French, Creole, Indian and Chinese traditions, all of which have evolved to take advantage of local delicacies.

Rice is the staple diet of many Mauritians, although it has to be imported. It is also the main feature of **Creole** food and, along with side dishes such as *brèdes* (a type of spinach), chutneys and pickles, is usually served with a curry, *rougaille*, fricassee or *moulouktani*. The latter, whose name has the same root as the word 'mulligatawny', is a curried soup made with small crabs and pieces of meat. *Rougaille* is made of tomatoes and onions sautéed with thyme, garlic, ginger and chilli (although the local version is made with the smaller *pommes d'amour* in place of tomatoes), plus a meat or seafood ingredient such as sausage, salted fish, shrimps and prawns. *Brèdes* is a bouillon made with the leaves and shoots of certain vegetables, while *vindaye* combines vinegar, garlic, saffron and other spices in the preparation of fish and meats.

Indian cuisine centres mainly on curries and their side dishes; biryani, a delicately spiced meat dish with a yoghurt-based sauce, is another favourite. Snacks such as poppadoms, samosas and chilli bites are often available from street stalls. Traditionally, spices in Indian dishes are crushed each day on a rock in the back yard, called a *roche carri*, so their full flavour is imparted to the food.

Chinese cooking traditions too remain faithful to their roots; familiar dishes such as pork fooyong and sweet and sour fish are common. The Chinese also eat sea urchins and sea cucumbers, sausage-like creatures which are often seen in the shallows.

Top of the list of local delicacies are smoked marlin, which tastes somewhat like smoked salmon, and heart of palm, which is either boiled or eaten raw in a 'millionaire's salad'. Venison and wild boar, along with smaller game, are

Below: *Fish, deliciously prepared in the Chinese way.*
Opposite: *The best of Mauritian fare, proudly presented.*

offered at many restaurants and are definitely worth trying. Octopus, prawns, shrimps, oysters and crabs crown a selection of tasty local fish that have intriguing names: *vieille rouge* ('old red'), *capitaine* ('captain'), *sacréchien* ('sacred dog'). Notable for their novelty value as much as for their refreshing flavour, carved pineapples (served lollipop-style on the fruit's stalk) are often sold by vendors at the roadside and on the beaches.

MARKET FARE

Gateau piment: fried dholl mixture containing chilli
Gateau bringelle: eggplant fritters
Bhajias: fried spicy batter
Gateau patate: fried mixture of sweet potato and coconut
Dholl puree: thin pancake spread with a tomato sauce.

Visitors in hotels are usually treated to a tame version of the spicy Mauritian cuisine. For the real thing, sample a few of the numerous excellent restaurants dotted around the island. The more adventurous can try the fare offered by the many roadside stalls in Port Louis and some of the larger towns – as opposed to the snacks sold by beach vendors, these stallholders offer more substantial food such as fried Chinese noodles, biryani or curry and rice. If you are staying in self-catering accommodation, try asking your cleaning lady to prepare your meals; remember to give her some advance warning so she can tell you what to buy. Fishermen on motorbikes call round in the morning selling freshly caught local fish. Alternatively, try the local *débarcadère* (fish-landing jetty) where fishermen bring in their catches.

Mauritius is self-sufficient in its production of many alcoholic drinks. Most popular is the thirst-quenching Phoenix beer and its stronger companion, Blue Marlin. Some palatable local wines, made from imported grape must, are available at a fraction of the cost of imported wines (although as duties on imported wine and whisky have recently been reduced, there has been a dramatic drop in the price of these products). A range of local spirit drinks such as rum (one variety, Green Island Rum, is exported), whisky, brandy, vodka and cane is also available. In addition to the usual soft drinks, some local non-alcoholic specialities include yoghurt-based drinks like *lassi*, and *alouda*, a syrupy streetside special made of milk, a gelatinous substance called Top Alouda, and flavouring. Finally, don't miss such tropical island drinks as rum-and-fruit cocktails, colourfully decorated with hibiscus flowers.

2
The North

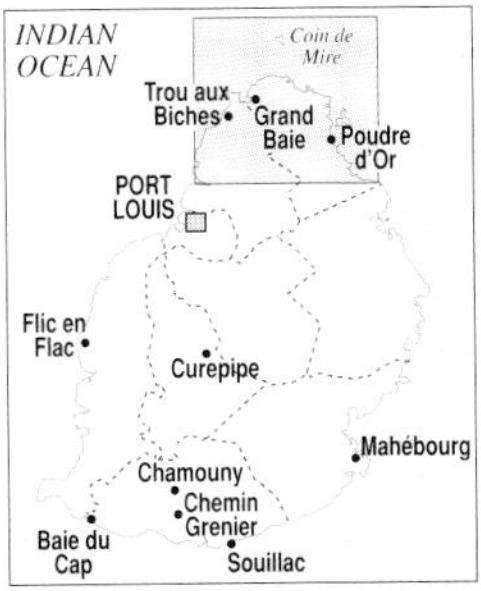

With glorious weather, a string of beautiful sandy beaches and still, clear lagoons as its prize assets, and the water-sport playground of Grand Baie as its focus, the northwest coast is the part of Mauritius most dedicated to the needs of the holiday-maker. Facilities are tourist-friendly, several top hotels have been built at or near Grand Baie, and restaurants here cater to a range of tastes. By contrast, the northeast remains relatively quiet; fewer bathing beaches adorn this stretch of coastline which, however, is worth a visit for its splendid views of the offshore islands. There is plenty to keep the visitor occupied, whether one opts for lazy days on the beach, sampling the host of more energetic aquatic activities available in the region, or taking excursions to the bustling cultural melting-pot of Port Louis and other parts of the island. Topographically, the north is the flattest part of Mauritius, rising gently inland through rippling fields of sugar cane, so the brooding presence of the mountains is not felt here as it is along much of the rest of the island's coast.

CLIMATE

Sunny skies are the draw-card of the region, which is fairly **sheltered** from the southeast winds; it is not as hot or dry as the west coast.

There is a risk of **cyclone** activity between December and late March. The **hottest** and **wettest** months are December to March; rainfall peaks in February. The **coolest** months are July and August, the **driest** October.

The Northwest Coast

Strung out between Port Louis and the tourist mecca of Grand Baie, the coast of the district of Pamplemousses has some of the best beaches on the island, and is an idyllic region from which to watch the sunset glittering on the calm waters of the reef lagoons and throwing into silhouette the fishermen and their nets.

Opposite: *The lure of the turquoise ocean at Cap Malheureux, the northern-most tip of Mauritius.*

Don't Miss

*** Water sports of all kinds at Grand Baie
*** Diving at Aquarium, Coral Gardens and Coin de Mire
*** A boat or helicopter trip to the offshore islands
** Bathing at Péreybère
* Maheswarnath Hindu Temple at Triolet

Baie du Tombeau

Doubt exists as to the origin of the melancholic name of this 'bay of the tomb'. One theory holds that it commemorates the tomb of George Weldon, the English Governor of Bombay who died here; a large monument was also erected by his wife and used as a landmark by passing ships for many years, though it is now long since gone. Equally plausibly, the bay could have been named in memory of the three Dutch ships which sank to a watery grave here in 1615.

Baie du Tombeau

The coastal resort nearest Port Louis, Baie du Tombeau, is more of historical interest than anything else, and is most famous for the wrecking of three of the Dutch East India Company's ships in 1615. Despite the relative security of Port Louis harbour where the ships sought shelter from a cyclone, they were torn from their moorings and blown to Baie du Tombeau where they sank. Pieter Both, then Governor of the Dutch East Indies, died on the *Banda*, now a protected wreck dive. One treasure-seeker, lured here in the 1970s by the wrecks and rumours of pirate booty, ruined himself in the hope of finding a fortune in these waters; some divers had more luck in 1980 when they brought up a haul of valuable old porcelain and a priceless astrolabe dated 1518.

More popular with locals and visitors from Réunion than with the sophisticated international tourist set, the area has a number of budget hotels and guesthouses. The beaches are pretty enough and protected by cliffs, but subject to pollution from nearby Port Louis harbour; swimming here is not advisable.

Baie aux Tortues

In the warm waters of 'turtle bay', giant turtles lived in great numbers until they were decimated by early settlers. Also known as **Baie de l'Arsenal**, this is where a French

arsenal was built to hold the ammunition needed to protect the colony. The picturesque ruins of the arsenal, destroyed in an accidental explosion in 1774, lie in a lush setting amid streams and waterfalls in the grounds of Balaclava's exclusive Maritim Hotel.

Overlooking Baie aux Tortues, **Balaclava** takes its name from the famous battle of the Crimean War. In days gone by this settlement was the site of a hospital for sufferers of scurvy, a powder mill, flour mill, lime kiln and distillery. For many years one of Mauritius' unrevealed beauty spots, it is now dominated by the luxurious Maritim and Victoria hotels, with the Oberoi and the Radisson nearby. Plans are afoot to establish Baie aux Tortues as a marine reserve, although some environmentalists have their doubts about the idea, and so far nothing has come of it. The waters here are good for snorkelling, and swimming is also possible.

A footpath leads from **Pointe aux Piments** on the northern side of Baie aux Tortues to the village of Pointe aux Piments, about 2km (1¼ miles) to the north. The name refers to the chilli bushes which used to grow in abundance here: the tiny red and green peppers are an essential part of Mauritian cuisine. The village faces onto a lagoon which is a favourite haunt of windsurfers from the nearby Trou aux Biches Hotel. Just north of Pointe aux Piments, the sandy beaches are interspersed by strips of black basalt rock which reach down into the water, creating fascinating rock pools; at low tide one can also walk to the reef.

Trou aux Biches

Unlike Trou aux Cerfs at Curepipe, Trou aux Biches does not have volcanic origins; the name alludes to a watering hole, which was once frequented by does. Trou aux Biches has now

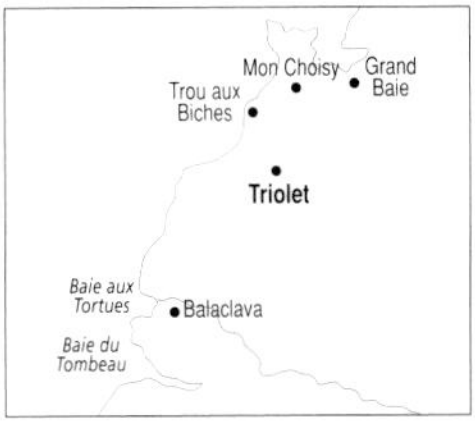

Period Boat Trips

The *Isla Mauritia* is a fully restored 19th-century sailing ship which is chartered out (along with a crew of eight, dressed in period costume) for pleasure cruises by Yacht Charters Ltd (tel: 263-8395). A romantic day's sail in this beautiful 32m (105ft) boat sets out from Grand Baie and heads for Baie aux Tortues, where it anchors at the secluded Anse des Filaos for lunch on board the boat.

Opposite: *Trou aux Biches.*
Below: *Harking back in time: the* Isla Mauritia.

grown from a simple fishing village into a prime resort – the extensive and top-class Trou aux Biches Village Hotel dominates tourism here, with the Casuarina Village Hotel providing a comfortable alternative. Young, jet-setting sunseekers are drawn to the long stretch of superb white beach, while water-skiing, windsurfing, yachting, trimaran and glass-bottomed boat trips are the order of the day in these waters. Snorkelling and diving are also a activities that are enjoyed here. Away from the beach the main attractions are the nine-hole golf course and tennis courts at the Trou aux Biches Village Hotel. Sunset cruises, the hotel casino, séga dances and other entertainment programmes round off the day's amusements in this exciting resort.

Above: *Shopping for designer goods at Grand Baie's Sunset Boulevard.*
Opposite: *Triolet's impressive Maheswarnath Hindu Temple.*

If you want to venture out of your hotel for some of your meals, you would do well to sample a few of the numerous restaurants situated here and just up the road in Grand Baie.

Further north you come to **Mon Choisy**. Its beautiful public beach, curving gently round to Pointe aux Canonniers and fringed by feathery casuarinas, is one of the best in the country. On weekends and public holidays the beach is packed; Mauritians come en masse to camp overnight and enjoy the simple pleasures of swimming in the balmy waters and cooking over an open fire.

A small Art-Deco monument by the roadside at Mon Choisy commemorates the first flight from Réunion to Mauritius. Undertaken in September 1933 by pilot Maurice Samat and his companion Paul-Louis Lemerle, the four-hour flight was successfully completed when they landed on a field across the road from the beach here.

Undersea Safaris

If you don't want to get your hair or feet wet but yearn to explore Mauritius' underwater treasures, book a trip on the semi-submersible submarine called *Nessie*. It has a special viewing chamber which enables you to marvel at magnificent coral reefs and marine life in complete safety. Previously the privilege of divers and snorkellers, a one-hour trip from Grand Baie provides a unique experience for people of all ages. Book through your hotel or tour representative.

The road leading to **Pointe aux Canonniers** is lined with flamboyants, which display a mass of red blooms in summer. Dubbed *de vuyle hoeck* ('filthy corner') by the Dutch because of the many wrecks which occurred on the nearby reefs, it was renamed by the French when they established a battery here. A lighthouse, built in 1855 on the site of the battery ruins and functional until 1932, stands as a national monument in the grounds of Le Canonnier Hotel beside the remains of the lighthouse keeper's hut and the historic cannons. Belying the point's stormy past and its less glamorous former function as a quarantine area for immigrants with infectious diseases, the lighthouse now houses a souvenir shop. The hotel's beach bar is used as an open-air disco at night. Next door, the exclusive Club Méditerranée allows non-residents the use of their many facilities and admittance to the nightclub show and disco for a fee.

COLONIAL STYLE

The Colonial Coconut is a charming, small hotel at Pointe aux Canonniers. Built in 1920 by the present owner's grandfather, the buildings are thatched, and the walls panelled with wood and ravenal. The hotel retains a true colonial ambience and houses an interesting collection of art, furniture and old books, acquired in the early years of the century.

It has an excellent restaurant, and the bar is notable in particular for its speciality, the 'mosquito sting' – a concoction of guava and mango juice, coconut, gin and rum.

Triolet *

A short distance inland from Trou aux Biches is **Triolet** which, at 7km (4½ miles), has the unusual distinction of being the longest village in Mauritius. It also has the greatest concentration of Indian inhabitants, and is a centre for Hindu festivities. The Maheswarnath Temple, built in 1857, is the largest Hindu temple in Mauritius: an imposing white structure which is ornately and colourfully embellished with moulded flowers and figures from this religion's mythology. A visit is well worthwhile; visitors must remove their shoes before entering the temple.

Riviere du Rempart Coast

Grand Baie and Péreybère ***

Protected from the southeast trade winds by Pointe aux Canonniers and Pointe Eglise, and with sunny skies almost all year round, Grand Baie has been able to add good weather to lovely scenery and become the most popular tourist area on the island. Some attempt has been made to control development, and buildings have been kept at one or two storeys in height. Luxury hotels abound here, each offering all sorts of facilities, and there are also many private bungalows that can be hired for self-catering holidays.

Grand Baie is a bustling resort with everything you could need during your holiday: car and bicycle hire, tour operators, shops, doctors, dentists and hairdressers. Banks have extended opening hours to cater especially for tourists. Boutiques, hotels and restaurants line the road from Pointe aux Canonniers. With holiday-makers aplenty and fishermen plying their wares at the **fish-landing station**, Grand Baie makes an excellent place for **people-watching**. Pedestrians should watch out for buses and cars that go tearing past, especially as the roads are uneven and the bends dangerous. Taxis may follow you as you walk along Royal Road, the main road through the village, insistently offering the use of their services.

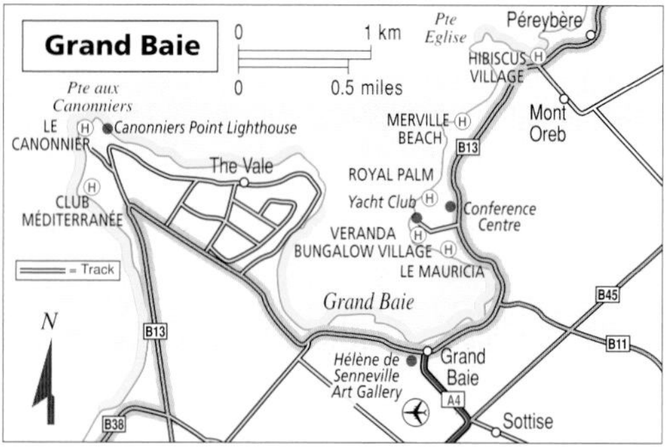

Most hotels offer all kinds of **water sports**, and if your hotel doesn't have what you want, the management should be able to make arrangements with independent operators. Grand Baie is also the yachting centre of the island and boasts an exclusive **yacht club** on the east side of the bay. Temporary membership is available for visitors, and boat repair can often be arranged. Join a sailing tour, take a gentle cruise, or charter a yacht for yourself. Some deep-sea fishing trips to the west side of the island leave from Grand Baie, as do a number of excursions to the northern islands. Water-skiing and windsurfing are also popular, and there are diving centres in the area (some are based at hotels, but are also open to non-residents). Unfortunately power boats have made the water somewhat polluted, and purists may prefer to swim elsewhere.

Several small, independent tourist agencies have offices on the main road, offering organized cruises or trips to nearby islands. Broadly speaking, though, they can be seen as 'fix-it' agencies – the middlemen of the tourist industry; ask them to arrange an activity that suits your needs and they should be able to find someone who caters for what you have in mind and work out the details for you, even if it is a picnic on an island, a cruise to Réunion or a helicopter trip. Certain boats can even be hired for a seaborne wedding, or for a very exclusive honeymoon.

Opposite: *The popular, upmarket resort of Grand Baie is the place to go for boating of all sorts.*
Above: *One of Grand Baie's many sheltered and pretty beaches; this one is in front of the exclusive Royal Palm Hotel.*

SELF-CATERING COOKING

Often the charladies at self-catering flats or houses are prepared to cook meals for a small fee. If you have an adventurous palate, this is an excellent way of getting to know Creole cooking. Identify broadly what type of meal you want, and your cook will let you know what you have to buy and in what quantities. If you can't speak French, get her to write a list for the shopkeeper, or if you are desperate, rely on sign language.

UNDERSEA WALK

A novel concept, and highly recommended for those who won't or can't dive, is the Undersea Walk. You can admire the amazing sights of the sea without spending time and money on a diving course. Participants are issued with weighted belts and head gear which allows you to walk and breathe on the sea bed; you do not have to be able to swim and there is no need to remove contact lenses or glasses. The guided walk operates from Pointe aux Canonniers, and is open to all but the very young; tel: 423-8822/263-7820.

A number of interesting little shops line the main road at Grand Baie. This is a fairly upmarket resort and on the whole you will find tasteful souvenirs here rather than mass-produced, cheap junk. Several clothing boutiques cater to the middle to upper range of the market. Some shops worth visiting are Canne à Sucre, Sous le Flamboyant, La Maison de la Laque and Ceuneau House which sells model ships.

Grand Bay Store and Store 2000 stock most requirements for self-caterers. Because of the emphasis on tourism, however, prices tend to be higher here than in other parts of the island.

Culture buffs will enjoy the small **art galleries** here (mostly on the main road) and in nearby Pointe aux Canonniers, such as Henry Coombes Gallery, Art Today Gallery, Galerie Hélène de Senneville and Galerie Raphael. In addition to permanent collections, some hold exhibitions of Mauritian artists' latest works. *Objets d'art* are mostly modern local pieces, many of which are in the naïve style. Bright colours reflect the heat and vibrancy of tropical lifestyles influenced by the sea. Some paintings pleasingly keep colonial style alive by concentrating on that era's architecture and customs. At the Ceuneau House showroom, situated between Grand Baie and Mon Choisy, top-quality model ships are displayed and sold.

Below: *An intricate and accurately crafted model ship, lovingly made near Grand Baie.*

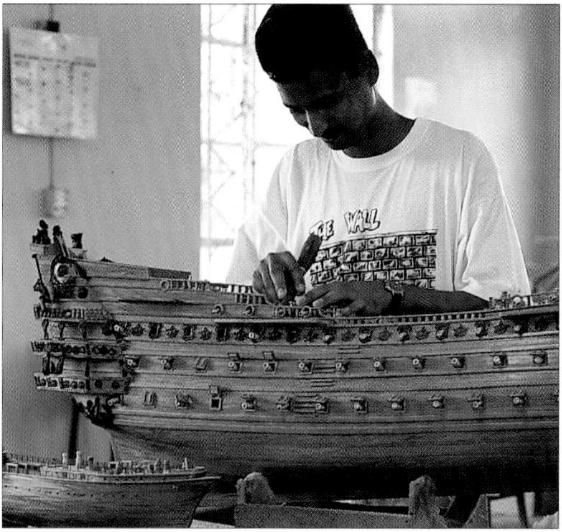

Night-life outside the hotel environment consists of a wide variety of restaurants and also pubs, cafés and other forms of outdoor entertainment, all located along the main street of Grand Baie.

If you can read French, look out for the monthly *Côte Nova*, which lists accommodation, shops

Above: *Feathery, green casuarinas edge the shores at Péreybère, said to be the best bathing beach on the island.*

and services, and what's on in the northern region. Aimed at the tourist, it is available at several points around Grand Baie as well as at the airport and in Port Louis.

Just north of Grand Baie you come to Péreybère, a small, sandy cove nestling between two headlands. With its deep but sheltered, clear blue waters, Péreybère is reputedly the best bathing beach on the island, and as with most of the other beaches between here and Cap Malheureux, it is lined with feathery casuarina trees. There are marvellous views of the northern offshore islands from this stretch of coastline; Coin de Mire's intriguing shape repeatedly draws the eye back to it. Pointe d'Azur provides a good spot for snorkelling.

Although it is only 2km (1¼ miles) from Grand Baie and very crowded at times, there are no large hotels here, nor is there the cluster of shops and restaurants that one finds in Grand Baie. Several guesthouses cater for the middle-category tourist market, however.

Best Diving Spots

- **Coral Gardens** off Grand Baie – pretty pastel corals, good variety of fish; excellent for night dives.
- **Aquarium** off Grand Baie – good visibility, and the many fish are used to being fed; depth 15m (50ft).
- **Merville Patches** in front of Merville Hotel, Grand Baie – a shallow, sandy dive with small reefs encrusted with coral; moray eels and trumpet fish abound.
- The **underwater crater** off Round Island.
- **Coin de Mire** – wall dive and reef dive in a cove near the island.
- **Whale Rock** off Trou aux Biches.

Cap Malheureux

Cap Malheureux or 'cape of misfortune' is the northernmost point of the island. According to local mythology, the corpse of Virginie (of *Paul et Virginie* fame) was washed ashore here after the wreck of the *St Géran* in 1744. Another of the Cape's misfortunes, from the French settlers' point of view, was the British landing here in December 1810, after which they marched on Port Louis and captured the island.

Above: *The church of Notre Dame Auxilia Trice at Cap Malheureux.*
Opposite: *First hints of dawn at Grand Gaube, a small fishing village in the northeast of the island.*

A small, red-roofed Catholic church, picturesque and much loved by photographers, sits peacefully on the headland with the large bulk of Coin de Mire dominating the background. Nearby is an unspoilt beach where the best views of this offshore island can be had.

La Maison, an exclusive little hotel here, was used in 1992 as a location for the film, *My Father the Hero*, starring Gerard Depardieu. In real life too, the guests in this elegant mansion are served by a team of butlers, chauffeurs, cooks and cleaning maids.

If you are staying in self-catering accommodation you may like to visit la Maison des Pêcheurs (literally, 'the house of fishermen') where fresh fish can be purchased.

FISHING

If you want to go line-fishing without joining an organized fishing excursion, local fishermen might be willing to hire out their boats and advise what types of fish are to be caught where. Try Articles de Pêche at Pointe aux Canonniers (tel: 273-7312) for fishing tackle.

Most big-game fishing is run by the established organizations; generally they will fetch you in the north and take you to the best fishing grounds which are off the west coast.

The Northeastern Villages

From Cap Malheureux eastward there are just a few isolated seaside hotels. However, it is pleasant to travel along the quiet coastal road by car, moped or bicycle.

Just off the road is **Anse la Raie**, a small cove named after a type of giant ray; found here by the early settlers it is, sadly, now extinct. The Marina Resort Hotel and the luxurious Paradise Cove Hotel are situated here.

The next settlement is **Grand Gaube**, a quiet fishing village with a public beach and a fish-landing station where fresh fish can be bought. The Grand Gaube Hotel

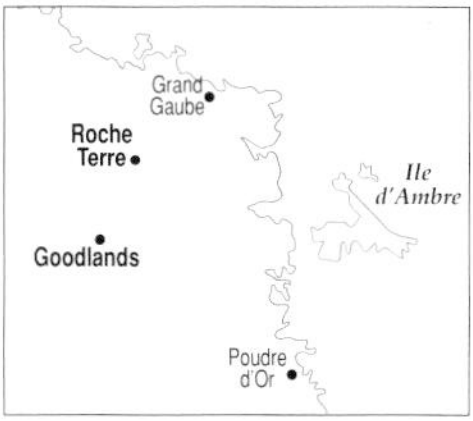

and the smaller Island View Hotel nearby mark the end of the tourist area as such. From Grand Gaube there is easy access to the nearby Ile d'Ambre, an excellent spot for a relaxing day trip.

To continue south along the east coast road you have to head inland to **Goodlands** first. If you are in the area try stopping off for a guided tour of the large Historic Marine model boat factory, where replicas of old sailing vessels are painstakingly constructed. There is also a large and brightly coloured Hindu temple here.

The inland road emerges at the coast again at **Poudre d'Or**. The golden sands of the beach here alternate with black basalt rocks, the result of lava spills, which reach out into the sea toward the reef. Poudre d'Or is home to the oldest religious building in the area, a Catholic church called Ste Marie Reine which was built in 1847; its bell predates it by nine years.

A few kilometres further south is **Pointe Lascars**, a peaceful fishing hamlet with a lovely little sandy beach. The shady cemetery on the point rather appropriately looks out to **Ilot du Mort** ('isle of the dead'). **Roches Noires** ('black rocks') is a tiny village on the coastal road leading to **Pointe des Roches Noires**. The long beach here extends all the way to **Poste Lafayette**; fishing is a pleasant pastime here, with cooling breezes, but swimming is not so good as the reef is fairly close in.

THE *ST GERAN*

At Poudre d'Or there is a monument to the *St Géran* which sank during a cyclone off the nearby Ile d'Ambre in 1744, while carrying spares destined for the sugar factories of Mauritius. The *St Géran* is the island's most famous wreck, probably owing to the legend that it was carrying the island's most beloved tragic heroine, Virginie. In 1966 the wreck was discovered by divers and was the source of a considerable haul of Spanish piastres; its bell was also brought ashore and is now displayed in the Naval Museum at Mahébourg.

Ile Ronde and Ile aux Serpents

With extremely difficult landing conditions, these two islands have escaped some of man's usual destructiveness, although goats and rabbits introduced as a food source destroyed the islands' hardwood forests. Ile Ronde is, however, still home to two species of palm that grow wild nowhere else on earth. Even here their existence is extremely tenuous, with only two Round Island hurricane palms and eight bottle palms left. Endemic animals include the multicoloured Telfair skink and two species of boa constrictor. Ile aux Serpents has a thriving bird population including the wedge-tailed shearwater, Trinidad petrel and red-tailed tropic bird. There are also the quaintly named noddy, sooty tern and blue-faced booby.

The coastal road crosses a lagoon where local smallholders grow *brèdes*, watercress and several varieties of spinach, as well as cultivating freshwater prawns and shrimps. Prior to the arrival of the Dutch the area was covered in ebony forest, but as the black wood was much prized, they and in turn the French felled the trees and exported the wood by the shipload to Europe. With the two largest sugar estates in Mauritius located here, agriculture is now the main activity in the region. There is not much evidence of traffic in this quiet area where many Mauritians have built their holiday homes.

The Northern Offshore Islands

These have all been designated as nature reserves and are thus protected areas, so you will need permission from the government if you wish to visit them. Some may be visited by boat or helicopter as part of day trips, mainly from Grand Baie. Ask your hotel to arrange it or visit one of the tourist agencies in Grand Baie; if you are not fussy, local fishermen might well be willing to take you out on their boats.

Coin de Mire ('gunner's quoin') is a bulky, wedge-shaped island which, with its highest point reaching 163m (535ft), dominates views from most parts of the north coast. It lies outside the coral reef, nearly 4km (2½ miles) from Cap Malheureux, although it seems much closer. The fault running down the west side of the island, le Trou de Madame Angon ('the hole of Madame Angon'), was used for target practice by the British navy during the 19th century. Coin de Mire is not protected by a reef, and from the shore, the waves can be seen dashing furiously on its rocky coastline, making landing rather tricky.

Below: *The striking form of Coin de Mire.*

Left: *Ilot Gabriel, on the left, and Ile Plate, two of the more accessible of the northern offshore islands.*

THE LEGEND OF PAUL AND VIRGINIE

Inspired by events surrounding the sinking of the *St Géran* in 1744 off the northeast coast of Mauritius, Bernardin de St Pierre wrote his novel *Paul et Virginie*. In this sad, romantic tale, Paul awaits the arrival of his lover, Virginie, who is on board the fated ship. As the boat flounders on the reef, he swims out to rescue her, but because the virtuous Virginie is too modest to remove her clothing to swim to shore, she drowns, and Paul dies of a broken heart. The novel was first published in 1788 and many editions have since been printed, making Mauritius synonymous with the fable in the minds of many Europeans. The account has assumed legendary proportions in Mauritius, and reminders of the tale and its many variations can be found right across the island.

The largest of the islands in Mauritius' northern waters, **Ile Plate** ('flat island') is covered by casuarinas and has a few beaches, as well as one of only two working lighthouses in Mauritius. It was originally a quarantine station for Indian immigrants who, it was believed, would infect Port Louis with cholera. Ile Plate is linked at low tide with its much smaller neighbour, **Ilot Gabriel**, and a coral reef almost entirely encircles the two islands. They are the least inhospitable of the northern offshore islands, and at less than two hours' boat ride from Grand Baie, are popular picnicking and snorkelling destinations with day-trippers.

Ile Ronde, 154ha (380 acres) in extent and much further out than Ile Plate, is the next island to the right on the horizon when viewed from the north coast. Despite its name it is not as round as its more distant neighbour, **Ile aux Serpents**, which, curiously, harbours no snakes – leading some people to believe that their names were the result of an early cartographer's mistake. Both are special nature reserves and casual visitors are not permitted. Diving enthusiasts may wish to explore the underwater crater, at a depth of 25m (82ft).

Set close to the shore just north of Poudre d'Or, **Ile d'Ambre** is remarkably intricate in outline and was the landing site of the 150 survivors of the *St Géran*. Excursions to this island can be organised through any local tour operator for walking, swimming, snorkelling, picnicking and even basic overnight camping trips.

The North at a Glance

Best Times to Visit

Weather is good **most of the year**. Summer is hot with mosquitoes and cyclones; visit in **April-October** for pleasantly **cool** weather. October is the driest time.

Getting There

By road: The highway skirts Port Louis and ends in Grand Baie; it should take up to an hour to get from the airport.
By air: Helicopter trips are costly, but spectacular aerial views make them worth while. Arrange such transfers when booking accommodation.

Getting Around

Taxis: The longer the hire time the better the deal. Many taxi drivers speak English and will act as guides. Ask your hotel to find a 'contract' taxi driver and suggest tariffs. Independent taxis park outside hotels in the morning; the drivers will usually offer a reasonable rate after some haggling.
The big **car hire** agencies are well represented but you may get better rates with local agencies such as Grand Bay Contract Cars (tel: 263-7831), Beach Car (tel: 263-8759), or Grand Bay Travel and Tours (tel: 263-8771).
Mopeds and **bicycles** can be hired in Grand Baie.
Buses serve the northwest well. Ask for a timetable from the airport information office. The northeast is more isolated and you may not be able to rely on public transport.

Where to Stay

Balaclava
Hotel Maritim, secluded, good snorkelling; tel: 261-5600, fax: 261-5670.
Victoria Hotel (Beachcomber), large luxury hotel, tel: 261-8219, fax: 261-8224.

Pointe aux Piments
The Oberoi
Luxury spa hotel, first-class cuisine; tel: 204-3600, fax: 204-3625.

Trou aux Biches
Trou aux Biches Village Hotel (Beachcomber), extensive resort hotel, casino and golf; tel: 265-6565, fax: 265-6611.

Mon Choisy
PLM Azur, gleaming white, compact French hotel;
tel: 261-6336, fax 261-6749.

Pointe aux Canonniers
Le Canonnier, three beaches, tel: 209-7000, fax 263-7864.
Club Méditerranée, big hotel; non-stop and entertainment; tel: 263-8509, fax: 263-7511.

Grand Baie
Royal Palm (Beachcomber), the cream of the luxury hotels; tel: 263-8353, fax: 263-8455.
Merville Beach Hotel, comfortable, older establishment; tel: 263-8621, fax: 263-8146.
Le Mauricia (Beachcomber), family hotel with huge pool; tel: 263-7800, fax: 263-7888.

Cap Malheureux
La Maison, gracious colonial mansion; chauffeured limousine and yacht for hire; tel: 263-8974, fax: 263-7009.
Paradise Cove Hotel, small, new luxury hotel; excellent restaurant and entertainment; tel: 262-7983, fax: 262-7736.
Coin de Mire Village Hotel, small hotel in pleasant setting; tel: 262-7302, fax: 262-7305.

Grand Gaube
Le Grand Gaube, good facilities, evening entertainment and excursions; secluded; tel: 283-9350, fax: 283-9420.

Budget Accommodation
Trou aux Biches
Casuarina Village Hotel, self-catering villas and rooms; tel: 261-6562, fax: 261-6111.

Pointe aux Canonniers
Colonial Coconut Hotel, *see* p. 43; tel: 263-8720/8171, fax: 263-7116.

Where to Eat

Trou aux Biches
Le Pescatore, excellent seafood; terrace with stunning sea view; tel: 265-6337.

Mon Choisy
Le Barachois, gourmet restaurant at Hotel Mon Choisy; tel: 261-6070.

Pointe aux Canonniers
Le Bateau Ivre, popular for French and Creole seafood; tel: 263-8766.
Le Carnivore, specializes in meat of all kinds; open-air with African mood; tel: 263-7020.

The North at a Glance

Le Navigator, stylish, with sea views from colonial house at Le Canonnier; tel: 263-7999.

Grand Baie

L'Assiette du Pêcheur, lovely view of bay from terrace; very good Creole-style seafood and meat; lively bar; tel: 263-8589.
Café de la Plage, popular for snacks, drinks and meals; tel: 263-7014.
Le Capitaine, local and Indian dishes – try the spicy seafood, served in a banana leaf, speciality! Live music, ségas; tel: 263-8108.
Le Grillon, delicious Creole and European seafood served. Snacks also available; Tom Cat Jazz Club thrice weekly; tel: 263-8540.
La Jonque, mainly Chinese, near the beach; tel: 263-8729.
Palais de Chine, attractive, beautiful views overlooking the bay; authentic Cantonese and Szechwan food; tel: 263-7120.
Sakura, exclusive and authentic Japanese restaurant; tel: 263-8092.

Péreybère

Hibiscus, seafood buffet/séga on Wednesdays, Creole buffet/séga on Sundays; served in open-sided bamboo building; tel: 263-8554.

Activities and Excursions

Major tourist agencies are represented at large hotels, local ones line Royal Rd, Grand Baie. Boat or helicopter trips to the offshore islands are highly recommended (permits from Conservator of Forests, Curepipe, tel: 675-4966).
Game fishing: Organisation de Pêche du Nord (Corsaire Club), Trou aux Biches, tel: 261-6267, is the largest. Otherwise try Sport Fisher, tel: 263-8358, at Grand Baie.
Diving: Paradise Diving, Grand Baie; NAUI-registered, well-equipped, good training, tel: 263-7220. Maritim Diving Centre, Balaclava, tel: 261-5600. Nautilus, tel: 261-6562, and Trou aux Biches Diving Centre, tel: 261-6562, at Trou aux Biches. Merville Diving Centre, tel: 263-8621, Diving World, Le Mauricia, tel: 263-7800, Islandive, Veranda Bungalow Hotel, tel: 263-8016, all at Grand Baie. The Cap Divers, Paradise Cove Hotel, tel: 263-7983, Anse la Raie. Sindbad, Kuxville, Cap Malheureux; tel: 263-8836.
Sailing: Grand Bay Yacht Club; tel: 263-8568. Facilities available to the public at the Casuarina Hotel, tel: 261-6552 and Trou aux Biches Village Hotel, tel: 265-6565, Trou aux Biches; or Merville Hotel, tel: 263-8621, Grand Baie. For yacht charters try Aquacat, tel: 262-8974, Croisières Emeraudes, tel: 263-8974, or Sindbad, tel: 263-8836, Cap Malheureux; Yacht Charters Ltd, tel: 263-8395, or Sinuhe Yacht Charters, tel: 263-7037, Grand Baie; Harmonicat, Pointe aux Canonniers, tel: 263-7839.
Ocean Pearl Charters; tel: 263-8899, does day charters to the northern islands or Baie du Tombeau. Also hires out cabin cruiser with crew and two six-berth cabins, ideal for weddings and honeymoons. Croisières Australes offers catamaran cruises to the northern isles; tel: 674-3695.
Windsurfing: Aquasport, Grand Baie, tel: 263-8686.

Useful Contacts

Grand Bay Tourist Agency, tel: 263-8411.
Grand Bay Travel and Tours, tel: 263-8771.
Lollipops, Péreybère, crèche for babies and toddlers; open 07:45-17:45, tel: 263-8717.
SSR Hospital, Pamplemousses, tel: 243-2661/2374.

NORTH COAST	J	F	M	A	M	J	J	A	S	O	N	D
AVERAGE TEMP. °F	79	81	79	77	73	70	70	70	72	73	77	79
AVERAGE TEMP. °C	26	27	26	25	23	21	21	21	22	22	25	26
Hours of Sun Daily	8	8	7	7	7	7	8	8	7	8	9	8
SEA TEMP. °F	82	82	82	80	79	77	75	75	75	75	78	80
SEA TEMP. °C	28	28	28	27	26	25	24	24	24	24	26	27
RAINFALL in	9	10	7	7	4	3	3	3	2	2	3	6
RAINFALL mm	235	243	189	171	104	86	83	76	49	48	67	156
Days of Rainfall	15	16	15	16	12	11	12	12	10	9	9	11
Humidity	79	81	82	81	80	78	77	76	73	72	72	75

3
The East Coast and Rodrigues

Away from the hustle and bustle of Port Louis, the northern resorts and the plateau towns, the east coast districts of Flacq and Grand Port seem quiet and isolated. Tourism is more of a going concern on the central part of the Flacq coast than along the Grand Port coast, which is relatively untouched by major developments: there are few hotels between Ile aux Cerfs and Pointe d'Esny, south of Mahébourg.

The Grand Port area is steeped in history: here the first Dutch colonists landed and set up a colony, sugar cane and Java deer were first brought onto the island, and more spectacularly, a battle was fought between the British and the French over who should rule this tiny but strategically important colony.

Some lovely beaches line the east coast, and strong onshore winds in winter make for good sailing. The Bambous Mountains dominate views inland from Grand Port Bay, where the land ascends steeply from the coastline; further north, rising behind the cane fields, they are a more distant feature of the otherwise flat landscape.

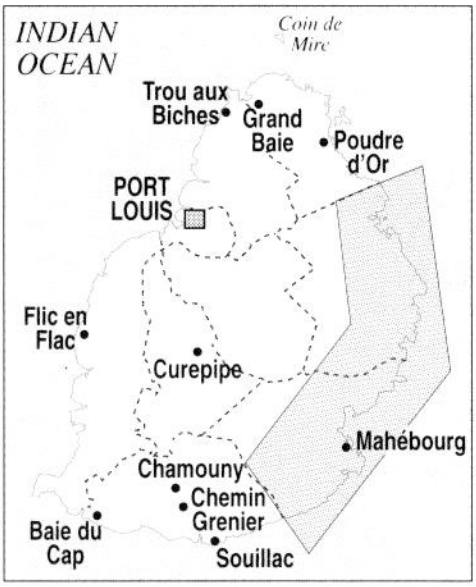

Climate

The eastern coastline gets the brunt of the **wind**, with onshore southeast trade winds blowing all year round; gentler summer breezes provide welcome relief from the heat, and stronger winter winds are appreciated by those who enjoy sailing.

The **wettest** time is from December to April; the **driest**, June to November.

The Flacq Coast

The Poste de Flacq Area

Pointe Lafayette, to the south of the village of **Poste Lafayette**, is prey to rough seas which crash through gaps in the reef; a lonely monument stands to the members of the Special Mobile Force who drowned during a training exercise in 1964. Inland lies the open countryside of **Plaine des Roches**, dotted with piles of volcanic rock

Opposite: *No costs are spared at the Oberoi Hotel, which has a charmingly tropical ambience.*

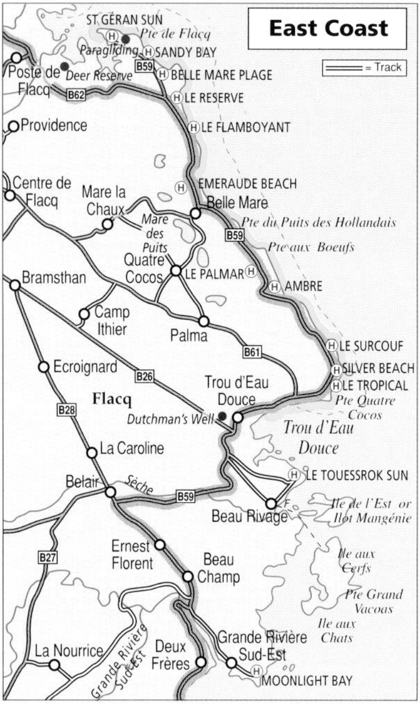

which, remarkably, were moved by early farm workers when the fields were cleared for cultivation. Along with similar heaps of rock elsewhere on the island, they are now being removed in the 'Prime Minister Derocking Scheme'. The area is not entirely given over to sugar however, and this is one part of the coastal flatlands where there is still some wild vegetation, as well as eucalyptus plantations.

The sea at **Poste de Flacq** is unsuitable for swimming and there are no beaches to speak of, but it is a good oyster-growing area, and oysters can sometimes be bought from locals at the roadside. A picturesque Hindu temple has been built by a local Indian family on Ile aux Goyaviers, a tiny island just off the coast which can be reached on foot at low tide. As you head south a large bay opens up to reveal in the distance the five-star St Géran Sun Hotel on the opposite promontory, **Pointe de Flacq**.

Self-caterers staying in this area can avail themselves of the daily market and other shopping facilities of **Centre de Flacq**, the main town in the region. If you are in the area, stop and have a look at the solid stone District Court House, which was modelled on the Scottish castle of the governor, Sir Arthur Gordon, and built here in the late 19th century.

Industrial Novelties

Several abandoned **lime kilns** dot the east coast. The early colonists extracted lime from coral by burning it, then used it in the construction of buildings and roads. The resourceful islanders found other uses for lime in the processing of sugar and enrichment of the soil.

The **Belle Mare sugar factory** is notable for being the first on the island to use steam power, in 1822; the man responsible for this was Adrien d'Epinay who, rather less progressively, was also an ardent campaigner for the retention of slavery.

Belle Mare

The highlight of the Belle Mare region for the tourist is the string of good swimming beaches, shaded by casuarinas, which extend south for 8km (5 miles) to Palmar and Trou d'Eau Douce. Mauritians visit this beach en masse on weekends and public holidays, camping under the stars and cooking on portable barbecues. For a superb view of the coastline, try climbing one of the abandoned lime kilns in the area, especially the well-preserved one just north of Belle Mare. For those with a taste for gambling, Belle Mare Plage and Le St Géran hotels have casinos. In the village, a marble monument stands in memory of the victims of the *Helderberg* disaster of 1987: the South African Airways plane was flying from Taipei to Mauritius when it went down, inexplicably, near the Cargados Carajos Archipelago with approximately 160 people on board.

Don't Miss

*** Exploring Ile aux Cerfs, with a meal at La Chaumière
*** Walking or hunting at Le Domaine du Chasseur
** The Mahébourg Historical and Naval Museum
* A drive along the coast to Grand Port

Trou d'Eau Douce and Ile aux Cerfs ***

First settled by the Dutch, Trou d'Eau Douce is now a quiet fishing village and secluded tourist spot. On the tip of a peninsula on the south side of the bay is Le Touessrok Sun Hotel; one of the island's oldest and most luxurious hotels, it is a favourite haunt of film stars and young European royalty. A short boat ride away is Ile aux Cerfs.

The island often features in aerial views of Mauritius – with its turquoise waters and pristine beaches it surely qualifies as a slice of paradise, not to be missed. Covered by casuarinas and scrub, and bordered by coves of powdery white sand, the island is 280ha (616 acres) in extent. The beaches are superb – if one does not appeal to you, just walk a short distance and find another secluded spot; despite the island's popularity the beaches are not that crowded. Note that the southwest corner of Ile aux Cerfs is not safe for bathing. It takes about three hours to walk around the island; if you want to explore, stick to the paths, some of which are patrolled by rangers.

The northern part is the most tourist-oriented. The land is leased from the government by Le Touessrok Hotel, which has built a boathouse, offering windsurfing, water-skiing, sailing, snorkelling and parasailing facilities, and two restaurants, catering for upmarket tastes, both formal and informal; one of them, La Chaumière, is an intriguing concept in design – perched on a hillside in a jungle setting, it consists of a series of thatched eating platforms rising above the treetops. Back on the beach, licensed vendors sell jewellery and clothing and there are a

Below: *Lazy days: relaxing in front of the luxurious Le Touessrok Sun Hotel.*

St Geran and Le Touessrok

Le St Géran and Le Touessrok Sun Hotels are two of the most luxurious hotels on the island – indeed the former was once voted the best resort hotel in the world. No costs are spared to provide guests with all the comfort and facilities they desire. Overlooking the bay on Pointe de Flacq, the elegant **St Géran** nestles in a tropical garden setting. Its vast swimming pool, dotted with floating islets and palms, winds through dining and bar areas. **Le Touessrok's** private rooms are built around an islet and linked to the main building on the tip of the Trou d'Eau Douce peninsula by a covered bridge. The hotel has recently been revamped, giving the Moorish buildings a colourful, beachy atmosphere. A magnificent swimming pool and proximity to Ile aux Cerfs more than make up for the lack of a good beach. Try the restaurants of either hotel for sumptuous meals à la carte or beautifully presented buffet spreads.

Above: *Looking down on the popular lagoon at Ile aux Cerfs, with the Bambous Mountains in the distance.*
Opposite: *Nestling among the mountains, Le Domaine du Chasseur is a private estate covering some of Mauritius' most pleasant countryside.*

few souvenir kiosks. There is a small deer reserve and some giant tortoises in an enclosure. At low tide visitors can wade to the undeveloped neighbouring island, **Ile de l'Est** or **Ilot Mangénie**; the gap is swimmable at high tide.

If you are not staying at Le Touessrok, take a boat from **Pointe Maurice**. Boats leave every half hour between 09:00 and 17:00 and tickets can be bought at the jetty.

Grande Rivière Sud-Est

A government-run ferry links Grand Rivière Sud-Est and the hamlet of Deux Frères ('two brothers'). The river ends in a striking gorge where, for a few rupees, young boys defy paralysis by diving into the water from a height of 30m (100ft). Further up the river are several pretty waterfalls, accessible mainly by foot.

Northern Grand Port Coast

The Grand Port area has had a long history, starting with the first landing of the Dutch in 1598 and the colonization of the island during the 17th century. The Dutch headquarters were abandoned when they left the island, and were taken over by the French in 1722 before they moved the capital to Port Louis a few years later.

Where the Bambous Mountains descend steeply to the sea, the road hugs the coast, passing **Pointe du Diable** ('devil's point'). This promontory is said to have been named when the compass of a passing ship suddenly went awry; the ship's engineer blamed it on supernatural forces. Cannons were stationed on the headland from 1750 to 1780 by the French to guard two gaps in the reef; the battery ruins now make a popular viewing point for both the mountains and the nearby Ile aux Fouquets.

From **Bambous Virieux**, it is relatively easy to visit the small offshore islands of Ile aux Fouquets, Ile de la Passe and Ilot Marianne (*see* p. 63). Local fishermen will take you out for a small fee, but take the precaution of checking whether the boat is seaworthy.

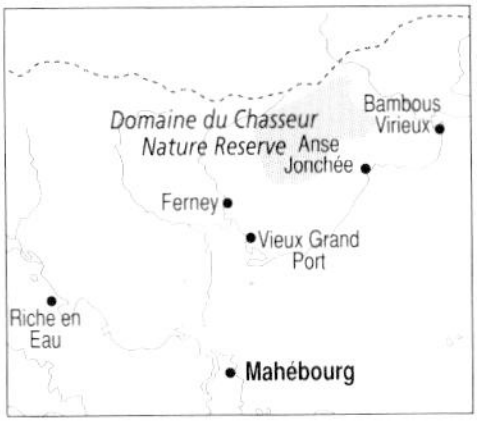

Le Domaine du Chasseur ***

A privately owned nature reserve developed recently on land of the Societé des Grands Bois, **Le Domaine du Chasseur** nestles among the Bambous Mountains on 1500ha (3700 acres) of land, and offers the visitor superb views over the sea and Vieux Grand Port. The Domaine will appeal particularly to anyone who wishes to hunt, as an area has been set aside specifically for deer and small-game shoots, offered throughout the year. Nature-lovers can visit for a relaxing ramble in the densely wooded and mountainous area, where wild orchids, ebony, traveller's trees, palms and other magnificent indigenous tropical plants grow. You may also see the rare Mauritius kestrel, a number of which have been bred and released here by the Government Aviary; they are hand-fed with dead mice every afternoon.

HUNTING PROSPECTS

For hunting, **Le Domaine du Chasseur** has no parallel in the region. Hunters can enjoy their sport throughout the year as hunting quotas are strictly controlled; the best time is from June to January. Experienced guides accompany you in four-wheel-drive vehicles, and you can hunt on foot or from the shelter of a mirador. The reserve has about 1500 deer and 500 wild boars, as well as rabbits, guinea fowl and monkeys. Although the deer remain the property of the Domaine, hunters can take home the head as a trophy; taxidermy and freighting can be arranged.

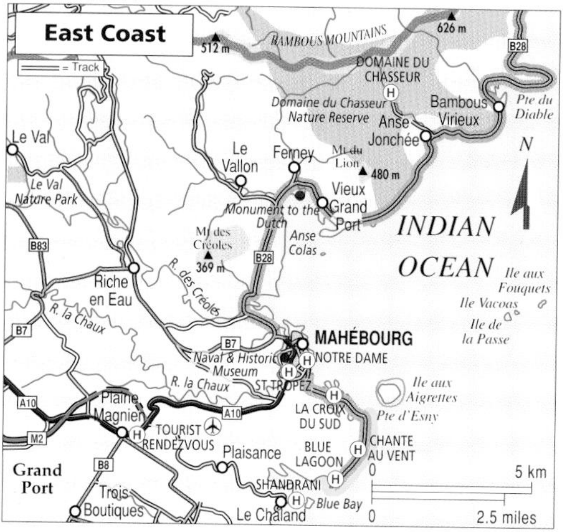

Vieux Grand Port

In the waters in front of the peaceful village of Vieux Grand Port, the British launched their first attack on Mauritius in August 1810 – the four-day battle was the only French naval victory in Napoleonic times. The remains of the English H.M.S. *Sirius*, set alight by its sailors to prevent the French from capturing her, lie in the waters here and can be explored by divers. The natural harbour of Grand Port was favoured by the Dutch settlers, but strong southeast winds created difficulties when ships wanted to leave, and for this reason the French, who settled here in 1722, abandoned it over the next decade in favour of Port Louis. These days local boatmen are often willing to take tourists from here to visit the offshore islands of Ile aux Fouquets and Ile de la Passe.

The **Ruines Hollandaises** at Vieux Grand Port are the remains of the original Dutch fort, shops and dwellings of 1638. In 1997 archaeologists unearthed finds which are now on display in the adjacent Fort Frederick Henry Museum.

With the profile of a crouching lion, **la Montagne du Lion** dominates the bay and the site of the early Dutch colony at its foot. It offers excellent views of Vieux Grand Port and the bay, and is a relatively easy and enjoyable climb which can be tackled in the space of an afternoon.

As the bay curves inland, you will see the entrance to **Ferney**, site of one of the oldest sugar factories on the island. Built in 1745, the factory ceased production in 1968. The gracious residence contains old maps, plans and drawings; although it is not open to the public, the house and gardens can be seen from the road.

The van der Stel Legacy

Sold into slavery in 1635 and freed three years later, **Adriaan van der Stel** went on to become governor of Mauritius in 1639. However, a far greater impact was made on the island by the two commodities he brought with him in the same year – Java deer and sugar cane. From these first supplies, viable stocks of deer have been built up over the centuries providing not only meat but also sport for hunters, while sugar has turned out to be the island's primary crop. Monuments to both have been erected near Ferney. Van der Stel's son, **Simon van der Stel**, was born in Mauritius in 1639, and he in turn gained a place in history as governor of the Cape Colony.

Mahebourg and Environs

One-time capital of the island, Mahébourg was named after the founding father of Mauritius, Bertrand Mahé de Labourdonnais. Today the largest settlement in the south, it has some importance as a fishing centre and is also the closest town to the airport at Plaisance. It has, however, managed to avoid a high-rise style of development and retains a 'laid-back' ambience. Despite having a pleasant waterfront, Mahébourg does not go out of its way to accommodate tourists. There are no hotels to speak of, although it does have a number of guesthouses which are popular with visitors from Réunion. Mahébourg was linked to the capital by rail until the railway was closed in 1964; the former railway station, Place de la Gare, has rather unglamourously been turned into a bus depot. The town's original road grid was planned by the early French colonists who left their stamp in the generous width of the streets.

Biscuits

Mahébourg has gained local fame for its ***biscuits manioc***, a Mauritian product made from manioc or cassava root. The factory making them, the Biscuiterie Rault, started production in 1870 and for a long time these were the only biscuits made on the island; it is the oldest factory in Mauritius. Guided tours are offered; tel: 631-9559.

Mahébourg Naval Museum **

Built in 1771 as the residence of a French sugar baron, the present-day Mahébourg Naval Museum was used as an infirmary for the wounded French and British commanders after the Battle of Grand Port in 1810. Ironically, they were forced to convalesce in the same room, and legend has it that they became great friends!

The house became a museum in 1950 and is run somewhat unimaginatively by the Mauritius Institute. Naval exhibits include a number of relics retrieved in the 1930s

Below: *The town of Mahébourg, showing the Cavendish Bridge over the river, la Chaux. The tiny Mouchoir Rouge and Ile aux Aigrettes lie close to shore.*

from the ships wrecked during the Battle of Grand Port, a cannon and cannonball, memorabilia of Robert Surcouf, 'King of the Corsairs', portraits of leading historical figures, and the bell of the shipwrecked *St Géran*. There is also a collection of period furniture, such as Labourdonnais' four-poster bed and two wooden sedan chairs used to transport important people in days gone by. Admission is free and the museum is open every day except Tuesdays, Fridays and public holidays. A model of a Creole house has been built in the garden; locally made handicrafts and souvenirs are sold here.

Le Val Nature Park *

At Cluny, about 10km (6 miles) northwest of Mahébourg, lies **Le Val Nature Park**. It is set in a valley amid the tributaries of the Rivière des Créoles, and surrounded by mountains. Le Val is an example of how sugar estates are diversifying into agriculture. The park covers 33ha (80 acres) and forms part of the huge government-owned Rose Belle Sugar Estate. As well as a series of fascinating walking trails through the valley, visitors may also find the estate's agricultural projects interesting: watercress, often used in Creole cooking, is grown in water fields, a few varieties of anthurium are cultivated in greenhouses for export to Japan and Europe, while an imported variety of giant, chemically treated freshwater prawn, *rosenbergii*, is bred here and can be eaten at the local restaurant. Children enjoy the deer enclosure and mini-aquarium, as well as the sight of sheep wandering around freely; fishing is also an activity that is offered; tel: 627-4545.

Opposite top: *Mahébourg Naval Museum.*
Opposite bottom: *Acres of anthuriums, grown under cover at Le Val Nature Park for export.*
Left: *Visitors strolling among the park's tropical vegetation can take in the many pleasant vistas through to the nearby Bambous Mountains.*

Plaisance

Originally a sugar estate, Plaisance is now best known for the **Sir Seewoosagur Ramgoolam International Airport**. The area's other claim to fame is the discovery by George Weldon, a British amateur naturalist, of a set of dodo bones in 1865. The reconstructed dodo can be seen in the Natural History Museum, Port Louis.

AIR TRAVEL

The first plane to land at Plaisance arrived in 1944, and regular flights started the next year. From 161 landings in 1955 the airport's facilities have expanded to handle nearly 6000 landings in 1993. Modernized in 1987, the airport is no longer like a hot and sticky rural bus-stop as it was in days gone by: it is now spacious, clean and air-conditioned and copes very well with the requirements of today's sophisticated travellers.

The Islands of Grand Port Bay

There are a number of small islands in Grand Port Bay, mainly dotting the edge of the reef. As with the offshore islands in the north, several endangered species of plant and animal have held out here, and some of the islets have been declared nature reserves.

Ile aux Fouquets, on the northern side of the bay, was the unfortunate home of the first French settlers of Rodrigues who, accused by the Dutch of stealing ambergris, were incarcerated there between 1694 and 1696. They survived their imprisonment by eating bird eggs. It now houses a derelict lighthouse (listed as a national monument) and numerous sea birds.

In the heyday of Grand Port, **Ile de la Passe** was an islet of strategic importance as it guarded the way through the reef to the harbour. Just before the Battle of Grand Port the British captured the fortifications, but continued to fly the French flag to trick the French into believing that it had not been taken. The ruins of its lighthouse and fort remain.

Opposite Pointe d'Esny, Pointe Jérome and the attractive La Croix du Sud Hotel is **Ile aux Aigrettes**. Half of this tiny island nature reserve has been cleared of exotic plant species and rats, giving endemic plants and animals a chance to flourish. There is a visitor's centre and guided nature trails are available.

Diving off the East Coast

The east coast is best for diving between September and May and although it can be dived in the winter months, visibility is not as good as in summer. Water and air temperatures are also cooler. One of the best summer dive sites on the east coast is the underwater pinnacle of rock known as **Roche Zozo**; east of Pointe de Flacq, this dive site has a maximum depth of 40m (132ft). **Lobster Canyon** is situated in a pass with plenty of big fish such as shark and tuna. With government permission, it is possible to dive in the bay of Vieux Grand Port and examine the wreck of the ***Sirius***.

Diving organizations include The Cap Divers Ltd, Belle Mare Plage Hotel, tel: 415-1083 Pierre Sport Diving, Le Touessrok Hotel, tel: 419-2451; Explorer, Hotel Ambre, tel: 419-2451; St Géran Diving Centre, tel: 415-1825; Shandrani Diving Centre, tel: 637-4301; Coral Dive, La Croix du Sud Hotel, tel: 631-9505.

Blue Bay

A resort area that has always been a favourite of Mauritian holiday-makers, the coast along the northeast side of Blue Bay and around to **Pointe d'Esny** is lined with bungalows. The bay is especially favoured for water sports, particularly yachting and windsurfing, and each winter, it is the site of regattas. A feasibility study has been made of the area with a view to declaring the bay a marine park. Oddly enough, there is no road skirting the bay, and the Beachcomber-owned **Shandrani Hotel** on the southwest side is accessed by a road running through the cane fields next to the airport.

Formerly Le Chaland Hotel, the very first tourist hotel on Mauritius, the newly refurbished 180-room Shandrani is situated on a peninsula facing Blue Bay and the **Ile des deux Cocos** ('island of the two coconuts'), and has the advantage of having three beaches on its doorstep. A pleasant walk from the Shandrani Hotel follows the coastline southwest to Le Bouchon.

Le Souffleur *

Once a major tourist attraction, Le Souffleur is a blowhole in a rocky headland jutting out to sea through which water is forced under pressure at high tide. With erosion, however, the effect has weakened considerably, although at spring tide 'the blower' regains some of the impressive force it had in the past, the water shooting some 18m (60ft) into the air. If you wish to visit Le Souffleur, you must get a permit from the police station at nearby L'Escalier.

Rodrigues

Unsophisticated and little known, the tiny volcanic island of Rodrigues lies 563km (350 miles) to the east of Mauritius. The island is only 18km (11 miles) long and 8km (5 miles) wide, and rises to a central ridge. The eastern part is especially hilly, while in the southwest the land flattens out into Plaine Corail. A coral reef surrounds the whole island, enclosing a lagoon which, in many places, extends 8km (5 miles) from shore.

The dry, windswept island was discovered in 1528 by the Portuguese navigator Diego Rodriguez. Although the Dutch first colonized the island, it was initially settled by French Huguenots fleeing religious persecution. Together with slaves, their numbers amounted to a modest 104 people in 1804. The British occupied Rodrigues in 1809, and from here they successfully launched assaults on Mauritius and Réunion the following year. It was administered as a dependency during the 158 years of British rule in Mauritius.

Nowadays, the small, Creole-dominated population of 34,500 consists almost entirely of Catholics, with a handful of Hindus and Moslems. Creole is more widely spoken than French, and it is rare to find an English-speaking islander. There is some dissatisfaction with the perceived neglect of the island by the Mauritian government, although there is a Minister for Rodrigues and the Islands in the cabinet and a Rodrigues-born MP for the constituency. The capital, Port Mathurin, lies in the north, but most Rodriguans prefer to live on higher ground along the central ridge.

The islanders' livelihood revolves around fishing and agriculture; fish – dried, salted and frozen – is exported to Mauritius, and octopus is a local speciality. Red meat and fresh fruit and vegetables are considered

Opposite: *A long, thin trumpet fish teams up with a school of yellow snappers.*
Above: *Fishing boats on Rodrigues are traditionally painted in bright colours. Their double-ended design distinguishes them from similar boats seen on Mauritius. Behind, the landscape is typically brown and dry.*

Don't Miss

*** a boat trip to Ile Cocos and Ile aux Sables
** beach-hopping south of Pointe Coton
** hiking up Mt Lubin for a panoramic view of the island
** fishing and diving in the southwest
* exploring Port Mathurin

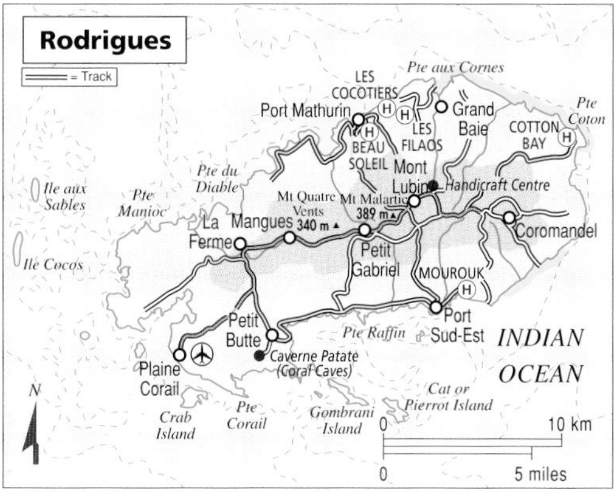

luxuries and mostly have to be imported, except for limes and hot peppers which grow in abundance.

Rodrigues has an unpretentious, primitive charm; with the opening of the luxurious Cotton Bay Hotel, the Hotel Mourouk at Pâté Reynieux and Escale Vacances at Port Mathurin, tourism is just starting to grow, although as yet the provision of luxury creature comforts has by no means reached the heights it has on Mauritius. Visitors enjoy boat trips and visits to the tiny coastal islands which bear such curious names as Booby Island, Cat Island and Hermitage Island. Other attractions include the Rodriguan séga tambour, which is faster and more primitive than its Mauritian counterpart, and browsing through local handicrafts, especially embroidery and basketwork made from local materials.

Rodriguan Wildlife

The disruption of Rodrigues' delicate, small-island ecology by people and introduced species has over the years caused the extinction of a number of life forms. Vast colonies of **turtles** and tortoises were decimated by early settlers and sailors, as they proved a delicious and easily transported food source; 10,000 were also exported to Mauritius and Réunion in the 18th century when a cyclone caused a food shortage. The **solitaire** went the way of the dodo (though its demise took more than a century), along with several other birds and reptiles. These days the **golden bat** is the only endemic mammal, and the **Rodrigues fody** and **Rodrigues brush warbler** are the only remaining endemic land birds; **sea bird** populations (including tropic birds, noddies and terns) seem to be in a healthier state, though.

The Coast **

The most beautiful beaches lie in the east and southeast. The roads have been improved in the last few years, giving access to unspoilt and isolated tropical island strands. **Pointe Coton**, with its lagoon, wide stretch of white sand, low coral cliffs and casuarina forests, is undoubtedly the pearl of Rodrigues' beaches; walking south from here one can stop off at the handful of attractive little coves on the way to the long stretches of sandy shoreline at **Anse Ally**, a white beach lined with coconut palms, **St François**, and **Baie de l'Est**. Further south the coast consists of smaller coves, there is less protective reef and the currents here are stronger; **Trou d'Argent** here provides a secluded bathing spot between two cliffs. The road to **Port Sud-Est** zigzags down from the centre of the island; watching local women gathering octopuses in the sand of the lagoon can be fascinating, and the village is also a good starting point for a trip to **Hermitage Island**. At **Rivière Cocos** one can take a boat out to the nearby **Cat Island** and **Gombrani Island**, the largest of the offshore islands.

A visit to the sand islands of **Ile aux Sables** and **Ile Cocos** is worth doing if you are interested in bird-watching, in particular the fascinating departure and arrival of the colonies of birds in the mornings and evenings. Visitors may not sleep over on the islands, and a permit is necessary, although the latter can be arranged through a boat charterer.

DIVING RODRIGUES

The lagoon around Rodrigues is twice the size of the island itself, and there are tremendous diving opportunities among the reefs and wrecks, in particular off Pointe Coton and Pointe Roche Noire in the east or Pointe Palmiste to the west. Equipment can be hired at the Cotton Bay Hotel and La Licorne Diving Centre in Port Mathurin. Henri Meunier, an experienced diver, takes divers out exploring the aquatic environs.

Coral Quarries, Caverns and Mountains ***

On Plaine Corail in the southwest is the **Caverne Patate**. The caves lie 18m (59ft) below sea level and feature strangely shaped stalactites and stalagmites; to visit it you will need a permit (free from the administration in Port Mathurin), and a guide will show you through its passages by the light of a flaming torch. In the same region is a fascinating coral quarry at **Petite Butte**.

For an overview of the island, try climbing **Mt Limon**, **Mt Malartic** or **Mt Lubin**; no point on Rodrigues is over 400m (1311ft) high, but climbs are steep. **Anse Quitor** and **Grande Montagne** became nature reserves in 1987.

Port Mathurin *

The capital, **Port Mathurin**, is a sleepy town most of the time, with vestiges of a more gracious colonial past remaining in its wooden administration buildings of 1873. Saturdays see the market come to life early in the morning, and once a fortnight the *Mauritius Pride*, the island's main link with the outside world, is welcomed in by crowds of Rodriguans, greeting friends returning from Mauritius, awaiting the arrival of goods, and eager to market their wares for sale there.

Below: *The sleepy town of Port Mathurin: as well as being the island's capital, it is the only port accessible to larger ships.*

The East Coast and Rodrigues at a Glance

Best Times to Visit

On the **east coast** of Mauritius, cooling onshore breezes make **summer** the most pleasant time. **September to May** is best for **diving**. **Winter** on the east coast is good for **sailing** – the winds are much stronger, especially in August. It is never cold, though, and the sea is warm enough to swim in all year round.

Temperatures on **Rodrigues** are warmer than on Mauritius, and it is more prone to cyclones, so **winter** is the best time to visit. The island's rainfall is low and unpredictable.

Getting There

The **east coast** is somewhat isolated, so best for those who prefer to stay based at their hotel without doing much sightseeing around the island. The east coast resorts are at most an hour's drive from the airport. Hotels arrange transfers; if you are not staying at a hotel, catch a **taxi** and negotiate the tariff before you leave.

Air Mauritius flies between Mauritius and **Rodrigues** daily; there are no other air links. The planes are all 46-seaters, so early reservation and confirmation of seats is essential; there is a 15kg (33lb) baggage allowance.

You can also get to Rodrigues by a 24-hour trip aboard the ***Mauritius Pride***; aeroplane-style seating, unless you book one of the few twin cabins. For cabin reservations contact Concorde Travel, La Chaussée, Port Louis, tel: 212-6002, fax: 212-2585; tourist class tickets can be obtained from Island Service Ltd, Dr Ferrière St, Port Louis, tel: 212-2894.

Getting Around

The **bus system** and **taxis** do not serve **eastern Mauritius** as well as the north. To explore the rest of the island, arrange for a **taxi** driver to drive you around for a few days, **hire a car** (try J.H. Arnulphy Car Hire, tel: 631-9806), or rely on excursions from your hotel.

Getting around **Rodrigues** is not that easy. The airport bus, **Supercopter**, ferries people between the airport at Plaine Corail and the capital; otherwise a limited **bus service** links most villages and Port Mathurin, but as it only runs from dawn till early afternoon, you may get stranded if you don't keep Rodriguan hours. **Jeep-taxis** are probably best for the tourist as the roads are poor; **hitch-hiking** is acceptable and relatively easy. **Henritours** and **Ebony** rent out vehicles, as do some guest-houses. However, Rodrigues is small enough to cover on foot if you enjoy walking.

Where to Stay

Pointe de Flacq
Le St Géran Sun, *see* p. 58; tel: 415-1825, fax: 415-1983.

Belle Mare
Hotel Ambre, big hotel on a cosy, sheltered bay; tel: 415-1545, fax: 415-1594.
Belle Mare Plage Hotel, plush hotel, golf course; tel: 415-1083, fax: 415-1993.
Le Flamboyant, 90 rooms, tel: 415-1037, fax: 415-1035.

Trou d'Eau Douce
Le Touessrok Sun, *see* p. 58; tel: 419-2451, fax: 419-2025.
Le Palmar Hotel, 36 rooms; tel: 415-1041, fax: 415-1043.

Anse Jonchée
Domaine du Chasseur, six thatched chalets with private terrace and fantastic views in a jungle setting; tel/fax: 634-5065, fax: 208-0076.

Mahébourg
La Croix du Sud, bungalow resort with good facilities, tel: 631-9505, fax: 631-9603.

Blue Bay
Shandrani Hotel (Beachcomber), smart hotel with most facilities; overlooking charming Ile aux Deux Cocos; tel: 637-4301, fax: 637-4313.
Blue Lagoon Beach Hotel, attractive hotel, good beach; tel: 631-9529, fax: 631-9045.

Rodrigues
Escale Vacances, Fond La Digue, Port Mathurin; tel: 831-2555, fax: 831-2075. Central, with homely atmosphere.
Cotton Bay Hotel, Rodrigues' first luxury hotel, on the island's best beach; tel: (095) 831-6001, fax: 831-6003.
Hotel Mourouk, new luxury hotel on the south coast; tel: (095) 831-3350, fax 831-3355.

The East Coast and Rodrigues at a Glance

Budget Accommodation

Trou d'Eau Douce

Le Tropical, charming little hotel on the bay, with direct access to the beach; tel: 419-2300, fax: 419-2302.

Le Surcouf Village Hotel, small, picturesque, studio-style hotel, views onto beach; tel: 415-1800, fax: 415-1860.

Pointe d'Esny

Villa le Guerlande, pleasant, self-catering bungalows; tel: 631-9882, fax: 631-9225.

Chante au Vent, four rooms, on the beach; tel: 631-9614.

Rodrigues

Les Cocotiers, the best of the island's guesthouses, on pleasant beach; tel: (095) 831-1800.

Where to Eat

St Julien

Chez Manuel, has a country-wide reputation for superb Chinese food; tel: 418-3599.

Poste de Flacq

Restaurant Monaco, authentic Creole food; tel: 413-2177.

Belle Mare

Symon's, Creole and Chinese, seafood a speciality; casual mood, beautiful farmland and mountain views; tel: 415-1135.

Trou d'Eau Douce

Chez Tino, Creole cuisine; splendid view of bay and off-shore islands; tel: 419-2769.

Restaurant Sept, Indian, Creole, Chinese cuisine, especially seafood; tel: 419-2766.

Ile aux Cerfs

Paul et Virginie, seafood served on the beach; tel: 419-2541.

La Chaumière, Creole food, expertly prepared with the freshest ingredients; served on thatched dining platforms in an attractive jungle setting; tel: 419-2541.

Anse Jonchée

Paranamour Restaurant, Domaine du Chasseur. Panoramic views and excellent cuisine, all fresh produce from the estate, venison and boar are the chef's popular specialities; tel: 634-5097.

Mahébourg

Restaurant le Phare, seafood restaurant; tel: 631-9728.

Port Mathurin, Rodrigues

Le Capitaine, doubles as a disco and eaterie, good seafood; Johnston Street, tel: 831-1581.

Le Gourmet, good Chinese lunches in local atmosphere; Duncan Street, tel: 831-1571.

Paille en Queue, first-class Rodriguan curries; Duncan Street, tel: 831-2315.

Activities and Excursions

East Coast

Don't miss a visit to **Ile aux Cerfs**; trips are organized by many hotels.

Go for a day's outing to **Domaine du Chasseur**, or spend the night there; a taste of their excellent cuisine is a must.

For **big-game fishing** contact Domaine du Pêcheur, part of Domaine du Chasseur, tel: 634-5065.

Rodrigues

The versatile **Henritours** will organize diving, trips to off-shore islands, and visits to the caves on Plaine Corail (and the requisite permits); also runs a taxi service; Victoria Street, Port Mathurin, tel: (095) 831-1635.

Rodtours has a similar range and rents out vehicles; tel: 831-2249.

Cotton Dive Centre, Cotton Bay Hotel; tel: 831-6000.

Useful Contacts

Rose Belle Hospital, tel: 627-4951.

Rodrigues Hospital: tel: (095) 831-1521.

EAST COAST	J	F	M	A	M	J	J	A	S	O	N	D
AVERAGE TEMP. °F	77	79	79	77	73	70	68	68	70	70	73	75
AVERAGE TEMP. °C	28	26	26	25	23	21	20	20	21	21	23	24
Hours of Sun Daily	7	8	7	6	6	6	6	6	6	7	7	7
SEA TEMP. °F	82	80	82	80	78	77	75	73	73	75	79	80
SEA TEMP. °C	28	27	28	27	26	25	24	23	23	24	26	27
RAINFALL in	11	13	12	11	8	5	5	5	3	3	4	9
RAINFALL mm	282	322	309	232	214	123	135	115	82	80	103	231
Days of Rainfall	16	16	17	17	14	13	14	14	12	11	10	14
Humidity	83	84	84	83	81	79	79	79	76	77	78	79

4
The South and Southwest

Considered by some to be the most beautiful region, the south coast and southwest interior are certainly rugged and dramatic. This undeveloped area is said to be reminiscent of what the island used to look like before tourism took off. As one travels west, the inland terrain is transformed from green cane fields to mountainous scenery, culminating in the Savanne Mountains and Plaine Champagne of the southwest.

There are several gaps in the reef along the south coast, and from Souillac to just past Le Souffleur the reef and the calm lagoons commonly found on the other coastlines are absent altogether. There are fewer safe bathing beaches, but the sight of powerful waves close by makes for a refreshing change, while onshore winds provide a measure of relief from the oppressive heat sometimes experienced elsewhere on the island.

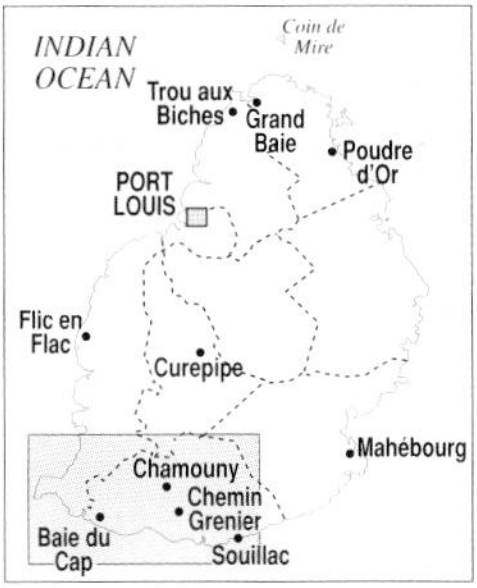

Climate

The coastline is subject to the edge of the southeast **trade winds**. These blow all year round but are at their strongest in winter. This area receives more **rainfall** than the west and north coasts, mostly during December to April. Temperatures are also **cooler**, especially in the mountains.

Savanne Coastal Belt

The Sugar Estates of the Southeast

The savannah grasslands that existed here until the 18th century gave way to the cultivation of sugar cane, and the road near the coast zigzags through the cane fields, crossing numerous rivers and streams and giving the occasional glimpse of sea in the distance.

Bel Air Sugar Estate was established by the French colonists in 1804. The factory itself is no longer in production, but palm-lined avenues lead to the owner's elegant homestead which is surrounded by terraced gardens and water-features, and visits for tea can be arranged.

Opposite: *The view of le Morne and Ile aux Bénitiers from Chamarel.*

Don't Miss

*** Plaine Champagne and the Black River Gorges Nature Reserve
*** Lunch at La Varangue sur Morne or Le Chamarel restaurant
** Chamarel Coloured Earths and Waterfall
* Horse-riding on le Morne Brabant peninsula

The main road from La Vanille passes through the **Union Sugar Estate** at **St Aubin**. The area also has several thriving anthurium nurseries where the waxy blooms are grown under shadecloth. Although they have been cultivated on the island for over a century it is only in recent years that these tropical blooms have become a major export commodity. The nursery of Corolla Ltd is open to the public with tours around its 1.5ha (3¾ acres) of flowers and its packing plant. There are lovely coastal walks in the area along the basalt cliffs.

Anthurium Nurseries

Warmth and humidity are ideal for the *Anthurium andreanum*, also known as the 'oilcloth flower'. The glossy blooms can be various shades of pink and red, or even a pale creamy green.

Each flower is carefully examined, and discarded if even the tiniest blemish exists. Local nurseries pack them in flat boxes that can be transported as hand luggage. The flowers lend an exotic touch to arrangements, and are popular in Europe and South Africa.

The anthurium's life-span depends on the ambient temperature: in ideal conditions they can last a month or more in water. To prolong the life of the flowers, refresh vase water regularly (add a teaspoon of bleach to it too), examine the stems for rot and every now and again snip off their ends.

Rivière des Anguilles

The main road crosses the river at the small commercial town of Rivière des Anguilles. Steep black cliffs rise on one side of the river; the other is much eroded. Typically, local women can be seen doing their washing in the river.

Just south of this town is **La Vanille Crocodile Park**, a popular tourist attraction established in 1985 as a crocodile-breeding enterprise. Apart from Nile crocodiles, originally imported from Madagascar, there are also snakes and geckos, tame monkeys, a wild boar (now domesticated!), giant tortoises and indigenous fruit bats. The colourful Telfair skink, endemic to Round Island, can be seen in a glass cage, while ponds throughout the park contain large goldfish.

Right: *Wooden fishing boats alongside Souillac's attractive little harbour.*

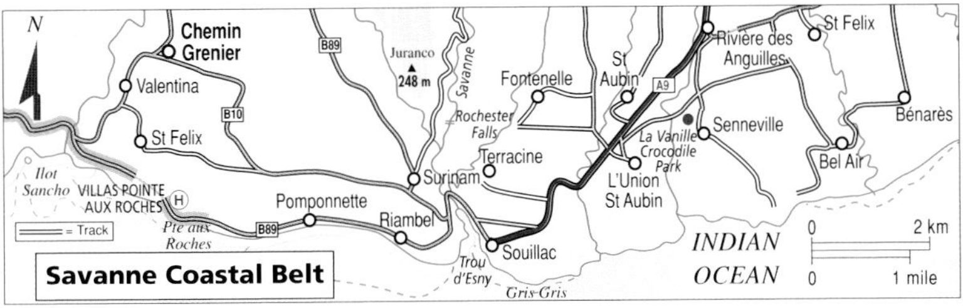

Savanne Coastal Belt

Guided tour groups are taken around the park every hour and told all about the crocodiles – for example, how all parts of the animal are used (even its front feet, which are sold as backscratchers!). A visit can also include a walk through a luxuriant forest filled with palms and other attractive tropical vegetation, and interspersed with freshwater streams (which flow into ponds that are unfortunately the breeding site of countless mosquitoes – take repellent or buy it there). The walk will be enjoyed by nature lovers but it is no place for high heels or prams. Small children may have difficulty seeing into the enclosures.

Souillac and Surrounds

The southernmost village in Mauritius, **Souillac** is also the most important settlement in the area and has a few tourist attractions, namely Gris Gris beach, the Robert Edward Hart museum, and the Telfair Gardens. The harbour on the east bank of the river, once a busy terminal where sugar was loaded on to boats to be transported to Port Louis, has now been developed into a charming little tourist attraction with the Batelage restaurant overlooking the pleasant waterfront.

Sheltered by two rocky headlands, **Gris Gris** is an attractive, empty beach with waves constantly crashing onto its golden sands. It beckons invitingly, but a sign warns that swimming is dangerous. The southern headland, **la Roche qui Pleure**, looks as though it's crying as the waves break over it. One whimsical explanation of the name Gris Gris is that the area was named after an early cartographer's dog; according to local legend, however, it is associated with witchcraft. In contrast, there is a rock formation in the distance called 'la Vierge qui Prie', which resembles an imploring madonna. Refreshments are available at the rather basic Gris Gris restaurant.

COASTAL WALKS

At Gris Gris in Souillac, an invigorating walk starting after the Catholic retreat leads along the rocky coastline, and there are enjoyable coastal walks between Pomponnette and Riambel. Those who wish for a change from the beaches will enjoy walking along the cliffs; reminiscent of the Atlantic coast with huge, breaking waves and whispering winds, the Souillac coast has an ambience just right for a Victorian tragedy rather than a light-hearted, tropical island fantasy.

A 5km (3 mile) walk from the deserted beach in front of the Bel Ombre factory heads eastward along narrow tracks through cane fields and banana plantations to Beau Champ; if you look hard you may come across coral caves in the cane fields.

ROBERT EDWARD HART

Although employed by the Mauritius Institute for many years as a librarian, Robert Edward Hart is best known for his poetry. Much loved by Mauritians, this half-Irish, half-Mauritian poet was the first president of the Society of Mauritian Writers and won acclaim for his poetry, written mainly in French. He won awards from the Académie Française, and was awarded the French Légion d'Honneur and the British OBE. No doubt Hart was inspired in part by the dramatic coastal setting in which he lived, and by the cultural diversity of the island; indeed in later years he became more and more attuned to Hindu thought and spirituality.

The museum of the poet **Robert Edward Hart** (1891-1954) is located in his home and contains a collection of personal belongings including an unfinished manuscript. Friends built the cottage from coral and presented it to him for his 50th birthday; overlooking the surf below, it is surrounded by lawns and shaded by huge trees.

Nearer Souillac are the **Telfair Gardens**, named after Dr Charles Telfair, a botanist who once owned Bel Ombre sugar estate to the west. The rocky cliff drops sharply to the sea and the fresh southeast trade winds blow constantly; shaded by banyans and huge Indian almond trees, the gardens also have views over to the historic Souillac cemetery. Although people are warned against bathing here, local residents do sometimes swim in front of the gardens, allowing themselves to be carried back to the shore by the strong currents.

A short way upriver of Souillac are the **Rochester Falls** on the Savanne River. Drive there, or enjoy the walk through the cane fields. Although not particularly high, the falls are notable for the unusual columns of black basalt rock over which torrents of water cascade; apparently the rapid contraction of lava caused by sudden cooling was responsible for the formation.

The splendid, deserted beach of **Riambel**, a village opposite Souillac on the other side of the bay, is protected by a largely unbroken coral reef and is safe for bathing. Its sandy shores lined with coconut groves and holiday cottages, the beach stretches westward for 5km (3 miles) to Rivière des Galets. **Pointe aux Roches** here has the only hotel between Blue Bay and Le Morne – just the place for those seeking peace and quiet rather

Below: *The Rochester Falls, near Souillac.*
Opposite: *The south coast at Baie du Cap.*

than entertainment. As there are virtually no other tourist facilities in the south, day-trippers may wish to stop off here for a meal or snack.

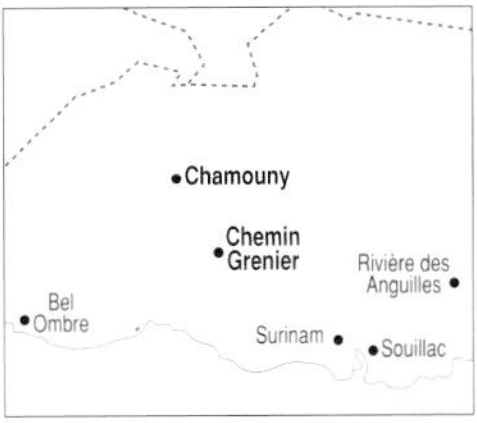

West of Pointe aux Roches

Ilot Sancho, the small, flat, scrub-covered coral island in **Jacotet Bay**, was used as a French military post until it was captured by the British in 1810. Rumours of treasure buried on the island, which can be reached on foot at low tide, are as yet unproven. Walking or picnicking in the peaceful environs of Jacotet River here, nature dominates one's impressions, as the lush carpet of sugar cane covering the rolling hills meets the rich blue of the sea.

At **Bel Ombre** the coastal waters are protected by coral reef. The Chateau de Bel Ombre is an attractive mansion built in the late 19th century; the plantation itself was established in 1776. Sugar used to be transported from the lagoon by boat along the west coast to Port Louis. Nearby, a monument commemorates the shipwreck of the *Trevessa* between Australia and Mauritius in 1923. If you really want to absorb the ambience of the area and are feeling energetic, try walking along the very scenic track from Plaine Champagne down to the coast at Bel Ombre, passing through beautiful forests and plantations, with glimpses through to the sea.

There is not much beach in the 4.5km (3 mile) stretch between Bel Ombre and the sleepy fishing village of **Baie du Cap**, although the water seems quite shallow for a long way out to the reef. Matthew Flinders, the navigator and explorer known best for his links with Australia, made the mistake of anchoring in this bay in 1803 on his return from the east; the hapless explorer was detained by the French for five years for the 'crime' of being British.

BASSIN BLANC

For **bird-lovers**, Bassin Blanc, which can be reached by car plus some walking from Surinam, is a water-filled crater whose top reaches 500m (1640ft). Superb views of the Savanne Mountains and the sea in the distant south are afforded from the edge. The crater's densely wooded banks create one of the few natural bird sanctuaries on the island. The scenic route here passes through tea plantations, with here and there, patches of wild raspberries. Just northwest of the crater is the spectacular Cascade Cécile; although access is difficult, the view of this narrow ribbon of water falling 150m (495ft) amid jungle vegetation is worth the effort.

> **OF SHIPWRECKS AND SURVIVORS**
>
> Survivors from the wreck of the *Trevessa*, which sank between Australia and Mauritius in 1923, landed on the beach near Bel Ombre after travelling across 1610km (1000 miles) of open sea for nearly three weeks. One of the two lifeboats stopped at Rodrigues, the other here on the south coast. Of the 16 people who survived the wreck, eight died at sea and one died the day after landing on Mauritian soil. The last biscuit ration and the cigarette tin lid used for measuring water rations are on display at the Naval Museum in Mahébourg.
>
> Another boat, the *Clan Campbell*, was wrecked on the reefs off the coast and sank in 1880. Two bells from the wreck were salvaged – one rings in the chapel at Baie du Cap and the other in the Chateau de Bel Ombre at meal times.

From here a winding road climbs inland to Chamarel and the scenic mountainous region of Plaine Champagne. The coastal road, however, hugs the precipitous sides of the narrow Rivière du Cap estuary, winding sharply round the rocky viewpoint of the Macondé promontory below which the boiling seas crash onto the steep coastline. A low-lying concrete slipway crosses the estuary: a number of bridges, vulnerable to rough seas during cyclones, have been washed away in the past. A boatman used to ferry people between the two banks of the estuary.

Le Morne Peninsula

Le Morne peninsula forms the southwestern tip of the Black River district; reputed to be the most African part of the island, this region's inhabitants are famed for their authentic séga dances and Creole traditions.

Le Morne Brabant *

The brooding bulk of le Morne Brabant mountain dominates the southwest and is visible from afar. At its foot is a flat headland with 14km (9 miles) of unspoilt coastline.

Le Morne has a sad legend attached to it. Because the peninsula was so inaccessible, it made a perfect hideaway for escaped slaves. When slavery was abolished in 1835, messengers were sent to tell the slaves the good news, but believing them to be captors, the slaves threw themselves off the mountain rather than be captured again. Access to their mountain hideaway was by means of a tree-trunk bridge, which apparently rotted away only recently. The area was prey to another tragedy when a ship was wrecked on the Passe de l'Ambulante in the reef during a terrible cyclone in 1772.

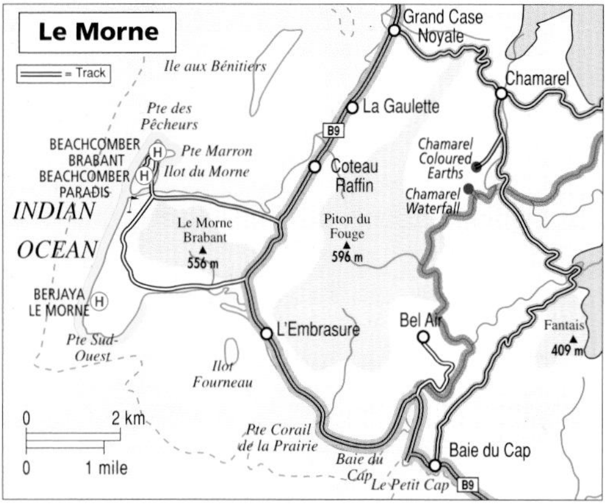

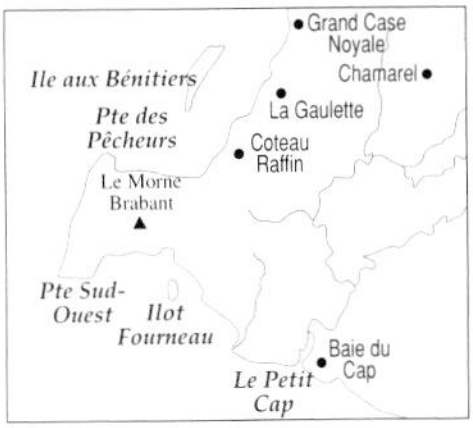

Left: *Le Morne peninsula's two Beachcomber hotels are a hive of activity; rising high above them is the bulky form of le Morne Brabant.*

The earliest tourist accommodation here consisted of 10 beach bungalows. The southern part of the headland has recently been developed with the building of the Berjaya le Morne there. Le Morne Peninsula is dominated by three hotels, Le Paradis, Berjaya le Morne and Les Pavillons hotels.

Although access to the peninsula by non-residents is discouraged, and permission must be obtained to climb the mountain, the peaceful, casuarina-covered parkland will appeal to horse-riders and walkers, and a beautiful, isolated public beach lies between the hotel developments. In the quiet, fish-filled bay south of le Morne lies the scrub-covered **Ilot Fourneau**; here the British colonists set up a military post to control the slave trade and the continued importation of slaves into the colony after the abolition of slavery.

Le Morne is also the centre for organised activities in this region. The Beachcomber complex has an 18-hole **golf course**, as well as excellent **big-game fishing** facilities; all three hotels here offer **diving** and a range of other **water-sport facilities** including parasailing, water-skiing, windsurfing, sailing, snorkelling. There are **casinos** at the Paradis and the Berjaya. The Beachcomber complex has nine **horses** and ponies; rides are accompanied by experienced equestrians who take you through

Golf

The Beachcomber Paradis Hotel's 18-hole golf course is situated in the shadow of Le Morne mountain. The course is 5809m (6350yd) in length and has four par 5s, 10 par 4s and four par 3s. Three holes run parallel to the beach at one point, while five cross a marina. Le Paradis Golf Club also has a practice green and nets, a driving range and a club house. As it lies in the driest part of the island, rainy conditions are not usually a problem. The club welcomes non-residents and offers golf clubs and trolleys for hire. Group and private lessons are available from two full-time instructors.

Dive Sites

At le Morne the best dives are at Casiers, Passe St Jacques, Needle Hole, Jardin Japonais and Grande Passe Sud. Fully equipped boats can be hired from Le Morne Paradis and Brabant Hotels. A recommended dive-site is that known as 'Bill's Murenes' or 'La Grotte des Murenes' which has a maximum depth of 30m (98ft) and features large, friendly moray eels.

cool casuarina forests in the shadow of the mountain, or for a gallop on the fine sands of the beach. Rides are tailored to the rider's ability and are charged per hour; lessons are available for those who prefer not to venture out. In summer, it is advisable to ride in the early morning or late afternoon to avoid the heat. With the ocean on one side and the dark, brooding mountain on the other, this is an experience not to be missed.

La Gaulette and Ile aux Bénitiers

The first small settlement north of le Morne is La Gaulette. Shells are sold by the roadside, and there is a branch of Shellorama shell museum and shop where shell, coral and jade jewellery can be bought. You may find local fishermen with the necessary equipment willing to take you out game-fishing. Alternatively, you could arrange a boat-trip to the nearby Ile aux Bénitiers, one of the larger of the offshore islands. Clad in coconut trees and bordered by unspoilt beaches, this crescent-shaped island takes pride of place in the pristine lagoon north of le Morne. Its few inhabitants make a living from fishing; rumour has it that part of the island may be developed with a hotel and 18-hole golf course.

Plaine Champagne

From **Case Noyale**, a road, recently tarred, winds up the mountainside to **Chamarel** and the plateau of Plaine Champagne, offering lovely views of le Morne peninsula and the lagoon. You may chance upon monkeys here, and maybe even a deer or two, as the adjacent savannah forms part of the island's southwestern deer reserve. Plaine Champagne offers the visitor a number of attractions, the first of which is the excellent **Le Chamarel**, a thatched restaurant perched on the edge of the plateau and commanding superb views of the lagoon far below.

Chamarel **

The area around Chamarel is a luxuriant, wooded plateau devoted to the cultivation of coffee. The Chapel of St Anne in the peaceful Chamarel village hosts a pilgrimage on 15 August every year for the Catholic feast of Assumption. The church also organizes a fair to collect funds, at which the unusual 'curry number two', considered a delicacy by the villagers, is served. And the reason for its name? Monkey, which takes second place to man on the evolutionary scale, is the main ingredient!

The attractive **Chamarel Falls**, dropping 83m (272ft) in thin strands through lush, tropical vegetation, can be seen en route to the Coloured Earths. For a closer view, the path to the falls is steep and slippery – only recommended for the intrepid explorer!

Various explanations have been given regarding the phenomenon of the **Chamarel Coloured Earths**. One theory holds that metal oxides account for the different colours: each of the seven shades has a different density, and they settle into their characteristic bands with gradual erosion; this is also why the colours separate out if you shake a tube of the earth (such as those sold at the entrance). Very little vegetation grows here, and the colours and undulating shapes have remained despite the ravages of wind and rain. The shades are quite subtle and it is hard to discern the full impact of a colour if you are standing on top of it; to appreciate the effect fully they must be viewed from a short distance away, preferably in full sun or early in the morning when the dew and rays of the rising sun combine to bring out the colours.

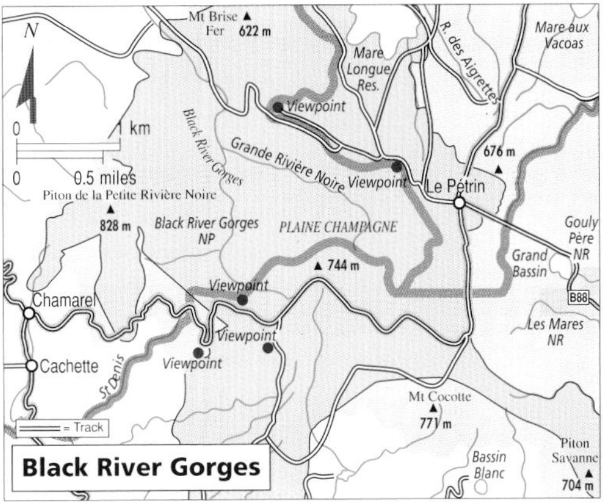

Opposite: *The restaurant and viewpoint at Chamarel.*
Above: *An aerial view of the unusual landscape at the Coloured Earths.*

BLACK RIVER WILDLIFE

The densely wooded Black River Gorges are part of the island's first national park, which has been established to protect the fast-vanishing ebony forest. Decimated by Dutch and French colonists, the ebony forests were further threatened by the settlers' need to clear land for large sugar plantations. It is only in the last decade or so that attempts have been made to preserve existing indigenous forest and encourage new growth. The gorge also provides protection for the rare pink pigeon and Mauritius kestrel which thrive in what remains of their natural habitat. You may also be able to see the national flower, the *Trochetia boutoniana*, a rare and delicate fynbos-type plant with a small, bell-shaped, carmine blossom. Apart from these indigenous treasures you might catch sight of deer, monkeys and mongooses.

A visit to the Coloured Earths is likely to be interesting rather than riveting; too many tourists have fallen for local hype and come away feeling disappointed. Note that there is evidence of coloured earth elsewhere on the plateau – keep your eyes peeled and you will see patches of it here and there. There is a small entrance charge although there are no toilets or refreshment kiosks. The Coloured Earths are open every day except public holidays and it is best to leave the area by 16:00 to be sure of getting out of the area by darkness. A new site offering 27 colours can be visited in the south at Bassin Blanc.

The Black River Gorges ***

On the narrow, winding road up from Grande Case Noyale to Curepipe, a short way past the excellent and beautifully situated **La Varangue sur Morne** restaurant, a fenced-in observation point allows visitors breathtaking views of the steep-sided Black River Gorges and a panoramic vista of the western coastline. The lovely **Alexandra Falls** are visible from a terrace reached by a series of stepping stones, and higher up, at Le Pétrin, is a bird observatory. A track runs from here along a ridge parallel to the Rivière Noire, passing through beautiful forested land overlooking the gorge. If you want to make a day's outing of it, you can follow the path which drops down to the river and runs alongside it almost all the way to the Baie de la Grande Rivière Noire.

You will need a permit if you wish to explore the area; camping and fires are not permitted. Take care when parking your car on the roadside and lock away valuables out of sight as break-ins have been known to occur.

Left: *Looking down the Black River Gorges.*

The South and Southwest at a Glance

Best Times to Visit

The south coast is cooler than the north and west, so this can be a good place to come in **summer**. Winter is likely to be much windier. Le Morne is very hot in the height of summer. Water temperatures are pleasant **all year round**.

Getting There

From Port Louis to le Morne along the **scenic coastal road** it takes about 45 minutes, and from the **airport** along the southwest coast between 60 and 90 minutes.

Getting Around

The most beautiful parts of this region are not accessible by public transport, so it is best to **hire a car** or find a **taxi** driver who can show you around for a few days. A **bus service** and **'taxi-trains'** link Baie du Cap and Souillac.

Where to Stay

Pointe aux Roches

Villas Pointe aux Roches, peaceful, unpretentious bungalow complex on the beach; tel: 625-5112, fax: 626-6110.

Le Morne

Le Paradis, twin hotels sharing several facilities on this scenic peninsula; renovated in 1995. Brabant is smaller and family-oriented; the action is at the Paradis with a casino, discos and beach parties; tel: 450-5050, fax: 450-5140.

Berjaya le Morne, new hotel on the south side of the peninsula; Oriental in style; tel: 483-6800, fax: 483-6070.

Les Pavillons, beautifully furnished, spacious hotel with five restaurants, weekly stage show; tel: 450-5217, fax: 450-5248.

Where to Eat

Pointe aux Roches

Green Palm Restaurant, the only restaurant in the area; Indian, Creole and Chinese fare.

Le Morne area

Le Domino, spectacular views, European, Creole and Chinese food; tel: 683-6675.

Café la Gaulette, simple but tasty Creole and Chinese food in a pagoda-style building, tel: 683-6755

Le Batelage, pleasant restaurant in refurbished warehouse overlooking the river in Souillac; tel: 634-5643.

Plaine Champagne

Le Chamarel Restaurant, perched on a cliff edge with views of Le Morne and the lagoon; fine European and Creole cuisine; tel: 483-6421.

Varangue sur Morne, chalet overlooking Plaine Champagne to the sea and Ile aux Bénitiers, French and Creole cuisine, recommended; tel: 483-6010.

Activities and Excursions

La Vanille Crocodile Park, near Rivière des Anguilles; open every day 09:30-17:00; tel: 626-2503.

Visits to **Chamarel Coloured Earths** and **Waterfall**, and **Rochester Falls**, are included in standard package tours from most tourist agencies.

For walks on **le Morne mountain** contact the Domino Restaurant, tel: 683-6675 or Le Paradis, tel: 450-5050.

Plaine Champagne for walks, fine views and fine food.

Black River Gorges: for a permit contact the Project Manager, Black River Gorges National Park, at the Conservation Unit, Le Réduit; tel: 464-2993, fax: 464-8749.

Big-game fishing: Beachcomber Fishing Club, Le Morne, tel: 483-6775, fax: 483-6786.

Private guides for **walking** and **climbing** trips can be arranged through Avho Limited, tel: 242-4052, fax: 211-0121, or the Beau Bassin Walking Group, tel: 454-0505.

SOUTH COAST	J	F	M	A	M	J	J	A	S	O	N	D
AVERAGE TEMP. °F	79	79	79	77	73	72	70	70	70	73	75	77
AVERAGE TEMP. °C	26	26	26	25	23	22	21	21	21	23	24	25
Hours of Sun Daily	8	8	7	6	6	6	6	6	7	7	8	8
SEA TEMP. °F	82	80	82	80	78	77	73	73	73	79	77	80
SEA TEMP. °C	28	27	28	27	26	25	23	23	23	26	25	27
RAINFALL in	13	13	12	11	8	7	8	6	5	4	5	11
RAINFALL mm	328	322	309	232	214	175	194	160	114	103	138	286
Days of Rainfall	16	16	17	17	14	14	14	14	10	10	9	13
Humidity	82	84	84	83	81	79	78	78	78	78	79	81

5
The West Coast

Mountains dominate the view inland from the coast of the Black River district, providing a striking, picturesque backdrop for the fishing villages and the savannah-clad deer reserves in the south and the cane fields further north. Rising high above the stretch of coastline between le Morne and Grande Rivière Noire, and the green and rural lands near the coast, are the Vacoas mountains, including le Piton de la Petite Rivière Noire, at 828m (2717ft) the tallest mountain on the island. Overlooking Rivière Noire is the Tourelle de Tamarin; further off to the north the Trois Mamelles and the Montagne du Rempart are visible in the distance. The waters are calmer along the southern stretch of coast, while near Port Louis there are several gaps in the reef where waves pound the shores and cliffs.

There is a lot to do on the west coast, which has a fair concentration of resort hotels devoted to water sports; indeed, the area is reputed to be one of the world's leading big-game fishing areas, and diving is also a popular pastime of holiday-makers here. Although the Black River district is the least populous on the island, there are well-patronized resorts with attractive beaches and quality hotels at Flic en Flac and Wolmar. Edged by some of the highest mountains on the island, and close to the scenic Black River Gorges and Plaine Champagne area of the southwest, it is favoured with good walking terrain too; nature lovers and conservationists will also enjoy visiting the Casela Bird Park and Black River Aviary.

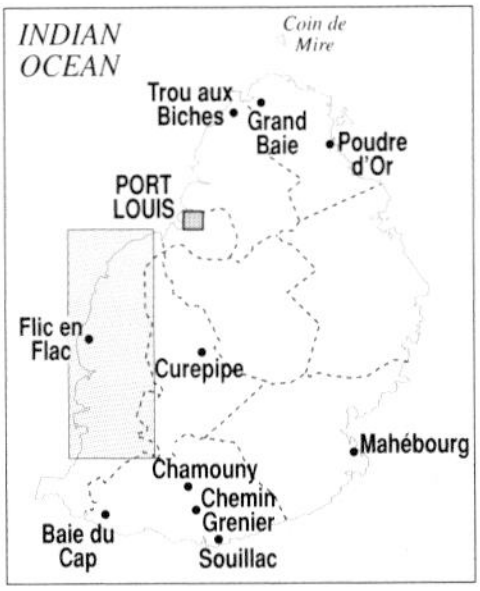

Climate

The west coast is the **driest** and **hottest** part of Mauritius, and lacks the benefit of cooling onshore winds. January to March are very hot but thereafter it is reasonably comfortable. The wettest months are February and March; not much rain falls during the rest of the year.

Opposite: *A boat rests in the calm waters at Flic en Flac.*

Don't Miss

*** Big-game fishing off the west coast
*** Diving on the coral reef
** A climb up la Montagne du Rempart
** The Casela Bird Park

Petite Riviere Noire

The village of Petite Rivière Noire revolves around deer breeding, fishing and, most notably, the collection of salt in its salt pans or *salines*. The salt pans are arranged in a series, with the salt water pumped to the top pans, then filtered down to the lowest pans where the salt is most easily collected after dehydration. The climate here is ideal for salt production as it is dry and hot. Almost enough salt is produced to satisfy the island's needs.

Students of the séga dance say that the way it is danced in this part of the Black River district is closest to the original and the least commercialized.

Black River Aviary

The government-run aviary near here is open to the public only by prior arrangement. Tour operators can arrange for a viewing of the aviary, whose specialist staff have been sponsored in projects which foster the breeding in captivity of such rare birds as the Mauritius kestrel, the pink pigeon and the echo parakeet.

In the 1970s these birds were recognised as being very close to extinction. From the mere handful of specimens known to be alive in the early 1970s, the aviary released over 300 Mauritius kestrels in the wilder areas of the island, such as a reserve on the Bel Ombre Sugar Estate, the Black River Gorges and Le Domaine du Chasseur. The aviary's captive breeding programme has ceased temporarily while the progress of the birds in the wild is monitored. Over 60 pink pigeons have been bred and these have been released in native forest such as that found on Ile aux Aigrettes near Mahébourg. Present breeding efforts concentrate on the rare echo parakeet, and the aviary is in the process of expanding its facilities.

Endemic Birds

There are only nine endemic species of bird remaining on the island out of an original 25. Most are struggling for survival, while the other 16 species, of which the dodo is the most famous, have sadly become extinct. The survivors are: the Mauritius fody or cardinal (*Foudia rubra*), the flycatcher (*Terpsiphone bourbonnensis*), the pink pigeon (*Columba nesoenas mayeri*), the cuckoo shrike (*Oracina typicus*), the echo parakeet (*Psittacula eques*), the Mauritius kestrel (*Falco punctatus*), the Mauritius blackbird (*Hypsipetes olivaceus*), the olive white-eye (*Zosterops chloronothops*), and the grey white-eye or pic-pic (*Zosterops borbonica*) which alone among these birds is common throughout the island, having adapted to a man-made environment.

Grande Riviere Noire

The Baie de la Grande Rivière Noire is the opening of the waterway which passes through the roughest areas of Mauritius. It is the most popular launching site for deep-sea fishing expeditions, and hotels dedicated to the needs of fishing enthusiasts have been established here.

Big-game Fishing and Diving ***

During the fishing season (October to April), game fish such as marlin, sailfish, wahoo, tuna and shark can be caught just 1.5km (1 mile) offshore, where the sea bed drops abruptly to a depth of over 600m (2000ft). Currents swirl around the foot of le Morne, creating a marine environment attractive to bait fish, which in turn draw game fish like marlin and tuna. There are a number of big-game fishing organizations offering fully outfitted boats for half- or full-day trips, depending on demand and the season. Of these organizations, the Centre de Pêche is the oldest and most established, while La Pirogue hosts the annual 555 Big-Game Fishing World Cup. Novices and children over 12 are welcome, and boats can usually accommodate five anglers; non-fishing companions can also go along. Once caught, the fate of the fish depends on its species and size: some are thrown back into the water if they are too small or too young, others can be prepared by the hotel's kitchen for the fisherman's

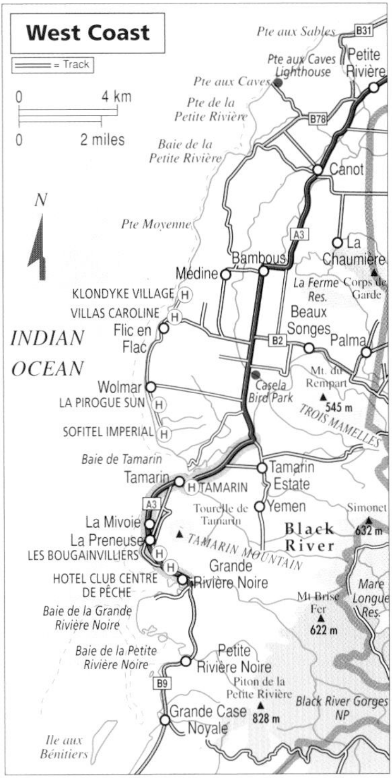

Left: *Well caught: a blue marlin proudly displayed at Black River.*

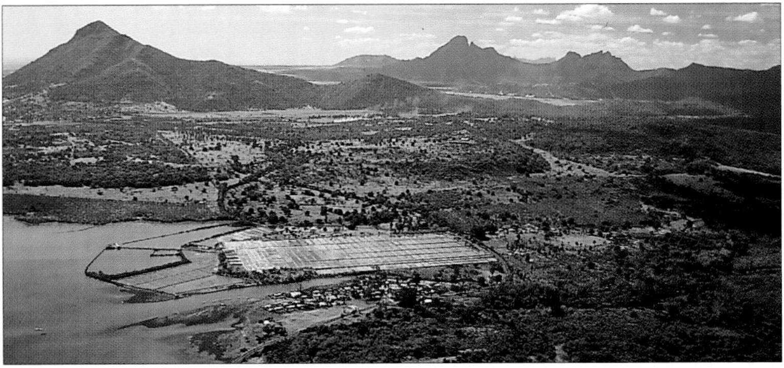

Above: *Salt pans against a backdrop of the Tourelle de Tamarin.*

dinner. Taxidermists are in contact with fishing organizations and will meet incoming boats, ready to take away certain types of fish for immediate preservation. Depending on their size, fish can be stuffed in a few days or sent on by freight several weeks later. Photographers are usually on hand to record spectacular catches, and if the catch is a big one, the fisherman's hotel is alerted by radio, and will generally organize a memorable reception.

Diving conditions on the west coast are fine throughout the year with water temperatures from 22-28°C (72-82°F) all year round. The most well-known dive site on the west coast is Cathedral Cave near the Sofitel Imperial Hotel at Wolmar. It features tropical fish, coral and lobster in an arched rock formation, which is recessed in a 30m (98ft) underwater cliff-face. Rempart l'Herbe, also known as Shark Place, is another favourite in the area, with small, tropical fish and game fish aplenty in the waters around this pinnacle; dives are done at about 40-50m (130-165ft).

SHELLS

Among naturalists Mauritius is more famous for its shells than for its fish. Over 1000 species exist in local waters, of which several are at risk of extinction. To protect this treasure-house of shells, it is illegal to collect them or export them without a certificate of origin. Do not buy shells or coral from beach vendors unless they can supply such a certificate. They may even try to sell you shells from the Philippines, imported to satisfy tourist demand; while this may stem the tide of destruction in Mauritian waters, it is not very healthy for the Philippine marine life. The Mauritius Institute in Port Louis has a shell collection which features a wide range of species.

La Preneuse

The small but prominent mountain of **la Tourelle de Tamarin** stands watch over the settlements of Rivière Noire, including La Preneuse and La Mivoie, as well as Tamarin further up the coast.

La Preneuse was named after a French warship which sought refuge from an English squadron on the nearby

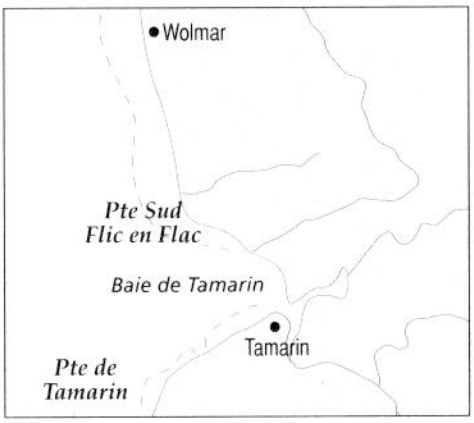

coast. Of historical interest is the Martello tower and museum, said to be Corsican in design and built as a lookout, for defence and for refuge. This listed monument has an underground well, a powder magazine on the ground floor, and on its first floor there was accommodation for soldiers. On the tower's open rooftop, cannons were once trained on the horizon. Other similar towers exist at L'Harmonie and Pointe aux Sables near Port Louis.

The main economic activity at La Preneuse is the smoking of marlin caught by the big-game fishing organizations nearby; there are also salt pans here. For shell souvenirs, try Shellorama between Rivière Noire and Tamarin (tel: 683-6704). The Cheshire Homes boutique and workshop further down the road near Tamarin also sells other souvenirs.

Tamarin Bay to Flic en Flac

Tamarin, situated at the estuary of the Tamarin River, was once famous as a surfing haunt, but with erosion of the reef, the waves are not as powerful these days. It is nevertheless virtually the only place on Mauritius' coast where one can practice this sport, and hotels in the area may hire out surfboards to visiting surfers. Tamarin is an

Below: *La Montagne du Rempart and les Trois Mamelles from Tamarin Bay.*

Above: *The large Sofitel Imperial Hotel at the resort of Flic en Flac.*

important salt-processing area, with huge salt pans dominating the landscape south of the village. Fishing, too, is a mainstay of the area, and fresh fish can be bought at La Maison des Pêcheurs.

From Tamarin to Wolmar, the main road heads inland for a little way before returning to the sea through green fields of waving sugar cane. **Wolmar** and **Flic en Flac**, just 2km (1¼ miles) to the north and linked by a coastal road, have been well-patronized resorts for many decades, although tourism and development of the area have now taken off here with the building of luxury hotels, including the Sofitel Imperial, La Pirogue, Sugar Beach and The Hilton. There are also a few small shops. The two villages share between them a 12km (7½ mile) stretch of white coral sand; with a shallow lagoon and a good measure of shade provided by the ubiquitous casuarina trees, and views southwards taking in the brooding le Morne mountain, Flic en Flac has the most popular public beach on the west coast. Beware of sea urchins, though, or better still, keep to the cleared and demarcated bathing areas.

FLIC EN FLAC

Several explanations have been offered regarding the curious name of this village. Some say that it is onomatopoeic – conjuring up the sounds and images of hands slapping on a goatskin drum, or feet squelching through mud in this formerly marshy area. Indeed, a more sober explanation is that it is another Dutch reference to the swampy flatlands, derived in a similar way to Flacq (*'vlaakte'*) of the east coast. Modern French argot would have it describing a 'cop' (*'flic'*) – an association surely not envisaged by the name's originators!

Casela Bird Park **

Situated just off the main road near the junction for Quatre Bornes and Flic en Flac is the **Casela Bird Park**. A lovely place for a peaceful stroll, the bird enclosures are set in 44ha (20 acres) of park-like gardens which boast a beautiful seasonal display of orchids. Some 2500 birds of 140 different species live in 85 aviaries, one of the highlights being the rare pink pigeon. There are also bats of all sizes; seeing these curious, upside-down creatures at close quarters, with their beady eyes staring at you, is a strange experience! The attraction of tigers, tortoises, monkeys and ponds with large goldfish will appeal to children. Beautiful views of the Yemen deer estate, nestling at the base of the Vacoas Mountains with the southwest coastline in the distance, can be enjoyed from the park's elevated position on the foothills of the angular Montagne du Rempart.

The park is open every day including public holidays from 09:00-18:00, October to March, and from 09:00-17:00, April to September; tel: 452-0693/4.

Three caves, tunnels which formed in the lava as it cooled and solidified centuries ago, inspired the name of **Trois Cavernes**, a nearby village. The caves now lie in less dramatic surrounds of cane fields, although they and the village have the splendid backdrop of **la Montagne du Rempart**. If you are in the area, you could try climbing this mountain; a short day-trip up this steep-sided peak will reward the energetic visitor with panoramic views.

CLIMBING

La Montagne du Rempart provides one of the few opportunities on the island for rock-climbing, as the route to the top involves negotiating a couple of vertical sections. Help is given in the way of bolts in the rock face, so one should take ropes; be careful of crumbly hand- and footholds. The view from the peak is certainly well worth the effort taken to get there!

Below: *The entrance to the Casela Bird Park, near Flic en Flac.*

Watchtower

Near **Pointe aux Sables**, just south of Port Louis, **La Tour Koenig** overlooks the Grande Rivière Nord-Ouest and the main road. Built in 1835 by the Koenig family, the tower was previously attached to a residential section which has since collapsed. Its immediate surroundings, inhabited by high society until the mid-19th century malaria epidemic, are now given over to light industry.

South of Port Louis

Between **Flic en Flac** and **Albion** further north there is no coral reef to provide a protective lagoon with safe bathing; the area has remained dedicated to the production of sugar, with a large sugar factory at Medine.

In terms of regional administration, the small village of **Bambous** to the north of the Casela Bird Park is the most important on the west coast. This busy village, complete with babbling brook and roads lined with flamboyants, was a lively community during the colonial years until the malaria epidemic of 1866, when its residents fled to higher ground. **La Ferme Reservoir** here at the foot of le Corps de Garde Mountain is popular with local fishermen.

The small coves at **Pointe aux Caves** are covered with a carpet of fine coral sand. The lighthouse here, built in 1904, is the only one on the mainland which is in working order. Views from the top of this 30m (100ft) high structure take in the mountains of Port Louis and the coast from the capital down to Flic en Flac.

Pointe aux Sables at the northernmost end of the Black River district is the closest resort to Port Louis. As such it is favoured by the capital's citizens as a weekend retreat although it is not a particularly pretty spot.

Below: *The countryside of the Bambous area, with le Corps de Garde, La Ferme Reservoir and the west coast beyond.*

The West Coast at a Glance

Best Times to Visit

Temperatures are pleasant in **winter**, water is warm enough for bathing. **Mid- to late summer** is prime time for **fishing**; make sure your hotel is air-conditioned or you will have uncomfortably hot nights.

Getting There

The most direct route from the **airport** is via the **highway**, turning off to the coast at Curepipe or Quatre Bornes; this route takes about an hour. It is pleasant (but slower) to follow the **coastal road**.

Bus services run from Port Louis to Wolmar and Rose Hill/ Quatre Bornes to Flic en Flac.

Getting Around

The roads have recently been resurfaced, but buy a good map to make up for the lack of road signs if you are driving. **Public transport** is regular and you could hire a **bicycle** for local trips, but these options would be limiting if you wished to visit le Morne or the mountains of the southwest.

Where to Stay

Rivière Noire

Hotel Club Centre de Pêche, *the* place for big-game fishing; tel: 483-6522, fax: 483-6318.

Rivière Noire Hotel, ideal for fishing holidays; recently rebuilt; tel: 483-6547, fax: 212-2611.

Wolmar/Flic en Flac

La Pirogue Sun Hotel, plush, established hotel with casino; tel: 453-8441, fax: 453-8449.

Sofitel Imperial, luxurious Oriental hotel with golf course; offers theme tours (such as cultural, historical, nature, architectural); tel: 453-8700, fax: 453-8320.

Klondike Village Vacances, studios/self-catering bungalows on the beach; lovely pool; tel: 453-8336, fax: 453-8337.

Villas Caroline, self-catering chalets overlooking beach and lagoon; excellent diving/deep-sea fishing; good restaurant; tel: 453-8411, fax: 453-8144.

Where to Eat

Rivière Noire

Pavillon de Jade, highly recommended for Chinese meals; tel: 483-6630.

La Bonne Chute, pleasant eatery, specializes in seafood with a European and Creole flavour; tel: 483-6272.

Flic en Flac

Sea Breeze, Chinese, very popular; speciality is Chinese fondue; tel: 453-8413.

Mer de Chine, tel: 453-8208, **Golden Horse**, tel: 453-8552, and **Ocean Restaurant**, tel: 453-8549, are all excellent Chinese restaurants.

Activities and Excursions

The following hotels are well equipped for **game fishing:** Centre de Pêche (tel: 483-6522) and Rivière Noire Hotel (tel: 483-6547) at Rivière Noire; La Pirogue (tel: 453-8441) and Sofitel Imperial (tel: 453-8700) at Wolmar. Beachcomber Fishing Club (tel: 483-6775) also does big-game fishing trips.

There are also several **diving** schools with concessions at the larger hotels: Odyssee Diving Centre, Centre de Pêche (tel: 483-6522), Rivière Noire; Sofitel Diving Centre (tel: 453-8700) and La Pirogue Diving Centre (tel: 453-8441) at Wolmar; Villas Caroline, (tel: 453-8450) and Klondike Diving Centre, (tel: 453-8335) at Flic en Flac.

For a change from the deep blue sea, outings can be arranged to the **Casela Bird Park**, tel: 452-0693/4, or the **Black River Aviary**; permission to visit the latter can be obtained from the Conservation Unit at Le Réduit, tel: 464-4016/4053, and Mauritours sometimes arranges group trips too; tel: 454-1666, fax: 454-1682.

WEST COAST	J	F	M	A	M	J	J	A	S	O	N	D
AVERAGE TEMP. °F	79	79	79	77	73	72	70	70	72	73	77	79
AVERAGE TEMP. °C	26	26	26	25	28	22	21	21	22	23	25	26
Hours of Sun Daily	7	7	7	7	7	7	7	7	7	7	7	7
SEA TEMP. °F	82	82	82	80	78	75	75	75	75	75	79	80
SEA TEMP. °C	28	28	28	27	26	25	24	24	24	24	26	27
RAINFALL in	8	8	5	4	2	2	2	2	1	1	2	5
RAINFALL mm	192	200	129	106	38	28	49	44	25	25	45	138
Days of Rainfall	10	11	7	8	5	4	3	2	3	3	3	7
Humidity	77	77	83	85	81	81	81	77	73	75	75	76

6 Port Louis and Surrounds

The capital city is one of the oldest settlements and still has reminders of its colonial past in its wide avenues and many gracious old buildings. It is also beautifully situated, cradled within the amphitheatre of the **Moka mountains** in the east and looking past the harbour out to sea in the west. To understand the soul of Mauritius it is essential to visit Port Louis. This is where East meets West and North meets South, and the old is woven in with the new. Here, three centuries' worth of French and British colonialism is counterbalanced by the oriental influences of China and India. The city is grimy and filled with car fumes. Rapid economic growth has created much poverty lately. Slums have grown in the suburbs and beggars crowd the main arteries of the town.

Port Louis first gained importance when the French East India Company, realizing the potential of its sheltered harbour and of the protection afforded by the mountains, adopted the town as its headquarters in the late 1720s in preference to Grand Port in the southeast. The capital and main port became firmly established in 1735 when Bertrand Mahé de Labourdonnais became governor and stamped his innovative brand of leadership on the administration and development of Mauritius.

In its heyday, the city was home to high society, with grand parties and balls, concerts and plays being held in the **Government House** (l'Hôtel du Gouvernement). At the same time opium dens and brothels sprang up side by side with the government and commercial enterprises, and in the latter half of the 18th century Port Louis

CLIMATE

Port Louis enjoys a largely **sunny** climate with the same rainfall and humidity patterns as those experienced at Grand Baie, although buildings tend to trap heat and **humidity**, causing sweltering temperatures in summer. This can make a visit to the city rather uncomfortable. Short, sudden, tropical **downpours** provide some welcome relief between January and April.

Opposite: *Port Louis, stretching from the Caudan Waterfront to the peaceful mountains in the distance.*

Don't Miss

*** A stroll down the Place d'Armes, with Government House and the Mauritius Institute and Museum nearby
*** The Market, for knick-knacks, herbal remedies and tropical island foods
*** The Chinese Quarter, taking in Jummah Mosque and the Lai Min restaurant
*** Sir Seewoosagur Ramgoolam Botanic Garden at Pamplemousses
*** Domaine les Pailles for a glimpse of the colonial past
*** The Caudan Waterfront and Port Louis Waterfront, new tourist resorts
** Panoramic views of the city from La Citadelle or Signal Mountain
* Champ de Mars on race day

became notorious as a base for French pirates and corsairs, who off-loaded their loot onto a willing market.

Port Louis was badly damaged by fire in 1816, and only half a century later successive malaria and cholera epidemics took a heavy toll on its population. This was a turning point for the city as many of the survivors were drawn to the cooler and healthier climate of the plateau, where subsequent generations have chosen to remain. The resident population of Port Louis is now close on 180,000; although commuters from inland temporarily swell the daytime population by 100,000, the city is deserted by night, apart from the complex at Le Caudan.

The Capital City

One's senses are assaulted here by the city's many sights, smells and sounds, while a feast of unfamiliar tastes awaits the visitor in market stalls and gourmet restaurants alike. Daytime Port Louis is crowded with people and maddening traffic, with drivers hooting incessantly as they make their way slowly down narrow, one-way streets, many of which still have the paving stones laid a century or more ago. Busy hawkers, loudly touting their wares at the side of the road in Chinatown and in doorways near the market, lend the town plenty of atmosphere.

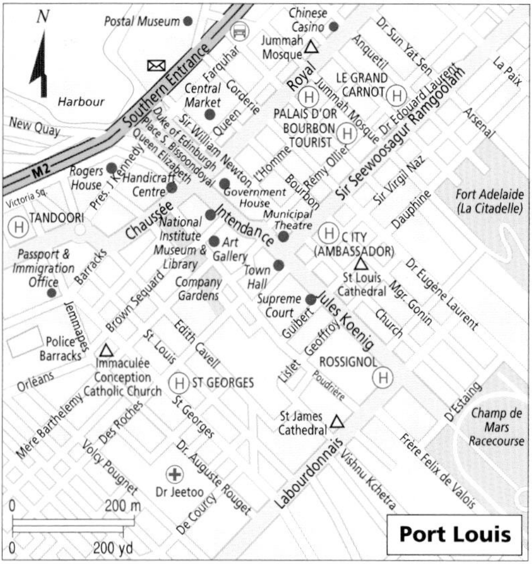

Elegant old structures and concrete cyclone-proof boxes stand side-by-side. Although there are some tall buildings, the administrative and commercial centre is free of true skyscrapers; this is changing as Port Louis has launched its 'free port' operating zone. The city's topography is constantly changing.

Left: *The Caudan Waterfront in Port Louis comes alive at night.*

The pavements are often uneven and not always pram-friendly, and little children on foot might find it quite a crush. Deep gutters, built to cope with torrential summer downpours, pose a further hazard to the unwary pedestrian. Walking around Port Louis in summer can be a very hot and thirsty activity. Many snack bars are not licensed to serve alcoholic drinks, so if you wish to drink alcohol, find out first whether it is possible. If you are planning a sit-down meal in Port Louis, it is advisable not to wait till evening, as many restaurants restrict trade to weekday lunchtimes.

Be warned that driving in Port Louis can be daunting: there are myriad one-way streets (albeit on a regular grid), and as some road names have been changed in recent years, they could differ from those printed on older maps. Street names like Eugène Laurent, Edgar Laurent and Edouard Laurent seem to have been chosen for the specific purpose of confusing the visitor! When the traffic is not in a jam, it flows fast and furiously so be alert if you don't want to be the target of a shaken fist or a few choice expletives – or involved in an accident. In short, driving here is not a relaxing experience, especially in the sweltering heat of summer or during a sudden tropical downpour, and a better solution is to hire a taxi for the duration of your visit to Port Louis, and tell the driver of your plans or ask him to suggest an itinerary. He should know

Pieter Both Mountain

Named after the governor of the Dutch East Indies who died in a shipwreck off Mauritius in 1615, this mountain is visible from Port Louis and the coast. It is unmistakable in form, its steep sides and pointed top surmounted by an enormous boulder which from a distance seems tiny and precariously balanced. The summit can be reached, and the last stretch has been fitted with iron bolts so that climbers may reach the top more easily, but it should only be climbed with people who are familiar with the area and local weather patterns.

The first man to reach the top was Claude Peuthe, in 1790. To solve the problem of how to secure his rope, he attached it to an arrow, shot it right over the rock, and anchored it on the other side.

Above: *The figure of Labourdonnais stands at the bottom of the Place d'Armes.*
Opposite top: *The Place d'Armes, leading up to Government House.*
Opposite bottom: *Sir William Stevenson.*

where to park and how to get from A to B with the minimum of fuss, and you could ask him to take you on a tour of the area.

Place Sookdeo Bissoondoyal***

Place d'Armes, officially renamed Place Sookdeo Bissoondoyal, is a grand entrance to the city as you arrive from the harbourside. Majestic royal palms that withstood Cyclone Hollanda in 1994 line the avenue, which is flanked by **Duke of Edinburgh Ave** on the north and **Queen Elizabeth Ave** on the south. On the strips of grass between the three avenues are several statues of historical figures; **Labourdonnais** commands the bottom end of the Place d'Armes, while the severe figure of **Queen Victoria** stands before Government House. Depending on the time of year, this symbol of British imperialism may somewhat incongruously be fronted by colourful panels depicting the celebrations of the various religious festivals. This is an attempt by the Ministry of Culture to express the acceptance of all cultural traditions.

At the bottom of the Place d'Armes is the harbour. This is still an active port, with many cargo and fishing vessels stopping over or based there; facilities were expanded in 1980 when a new container terminal was built on reclaimed land. In addition, the **Caudan Waterfront** and Port Louis Waterfront have enlivened the city. The complex has been built along the lines of similar developments in San Francisco and Cape Town. This exciting project has provided the waterfront with several restaurants and cinemas, a large shopping area, casino, hotel, offices and an entertainment plaza, and incorporates some of the city's oldest buildings (such as the old **British Customs House** and several warehouses of the 18th century). Various cruises from Port Louis harbour are available.

A Capital Name

Port Louis' original name was the Dutch '**Noordwester Haven**'; translating this, and following unimaginatively in the same vein as Port Sud-Est (now Mahébourg), the town was called '**Port Nord-Ouest**' by the early French settlers. This name endured until at least 1735, despite officially changing in 1722 to '**Port Louis**' in honour of France's King Louis XV (1715-1771). As the monarchy fell out of favour, the capital was renamed '**Port Napoleon**' in 1806, but reverted to '**Port Louis**' when it came under British control.

Several grand, 19th-century buildings line the Place d'Armes, with the elegant, dove-grey **Government House**, the oldest building on the island, in prime position at the top of the avenue. The original structure, completed in 1738, consisted of a ground floor and first floor; another was later added in the same style by Governor Decaen in 1809, although the building remained modest in size. The façade is given depth by its typically colonial verandahs and delicate colonnades which run the length of every floor, and the whole building is surrounded by large, shade-giving trees. Originally the winter residence of the governors of the colony, both French and English, Government House would attract all the glittering personages of high society each winter. It still contains several valuable pieces of period furniture and paintings of prominent figures from Britain's colonial past, and is used to house some administrative offices and committee rooms. It is not open to the public, however, and the Mauritian government is no longer based here; the Legislative Assembly now sits in a building just behind.

Across the road to the south of Government House is the **Mauritius Institute and Museum**, established in 1880. The **Natural History Museum** houses a reconstructed dodo, as well as the bones of a dodo skeleton found at Plaisance and other relics of natural history such as rare shells and fish.

FIGURES OF THE PAST

Walking up the Place d'Armes and into the Company Gardens, you will encounter a number of statues of people who have made important contributions to Mauritius: **Mahé de Labourdonnais** (1699-1753); **Emmanuel Anquetil** (1885-1946), trade unionist, and **Renganaden Seeneevassen** (1910-58), lawyer and politician; **Sir John Pope Hennessy** (1834-91), British governor who supported Mauritian independence; he was tried in London and successfully defended by **Sir William Newton** (1842-1915), a Mauritian lawyer who supported political reform; **Queen Victoria** (1819-1901); **Adrien d'Epinay** (1794-1840), lawyer who campaigned against the abolition of slavery and won compensation for slave-owners after emancipation; founded *Le Cernéen*; **Rémy Ollier** (1816-45), politician who campaigned for Creole political rights and social justice; **Manilall Doctor** (1881-1956), Indian advocate, sent by Gandhi to help the political organization of the indentured Indian labourers; **Brown Sequard** (1817-94), a scientist, and **Léoville l'Homme** (1857-1928), a poet and journalist.

Objects salvaged from the island's many shipwrecks are exhibited in the **Historical Museum**, and include historical drawings, stamps, maps and paintings. On the second floor, the public **Reference Library** has a collection of over 50,000 books which includes a comprehensive section devoted to the Mascarene Archipelago.

The entire complex is set next to the **Company Gardens** (Jardins de la Compagnie). In early colonial times this was a swampy burial ground; it became in turn a revictualling garden for ships calling at port and the site of the city's market, and it now provides a welcome 'green lung' in the heart of the capital, with some old trees, including a baobab of Indian origin, several bottle palms and a giant banyan. The gardens are not always a tranquil spot, though, as strikes and demonstrations are sometimes held there. There are a number of statues celebrating the lives of Mauritian dignitaries of years gone by.

The Market ***

Although it was badly hit by fire in 1981, the market has been operating on the same site between Queen and Farquhar St since 1828, and the original gates of 1844 still stand, with the regal initials, 'VR', worked into the intricate wrought iron. Here, the heady mix of cultures is colourful, noisy and at times a little bewildering: brash colours, mysterious fragrances, new tastes and unexpected sights combine to provide a unique experience.

Right: *The gates of the Port Louis market.*
Opposite: *A hopeful stall-holder displays his wares in the Port Louis market.*

Nonperishable goods are sold on the inland side of the market: gaudy earrings, plastic dodos, basketware, tiger balm for headaches, vividly coloured cosmetic powders, bejewelled turbans worn by the groom at Hindu weddings, famous-name T-shirts (though not the genuine article!) and beautifully embroidered tablecloths. Several stalls only close after the regular tourist groups have done the rounds, but if you do want to see all the stalls make sure you make an early start.

All manner of herbs for cooking as well as medicinal use are sold at the market. Some stallholders specialize in herbs said to cure afflictions from incontinence and haemorrhoids to sadness or even 'overheating' (*échauffement*). The herbs, sold by the handful, should be infused in boiling water. Although some people swear by them, their sale is not sanctioned by the health authorities.

The side of the market closest to the harbour is for perishables. In the steamy confines of this section you can take your pick of boxes, jars, neatly arranged piles and pyramids of pungent dried fish, brown-skinned litchis, pineapples, aubergines, watermelons, scarlet *pommes d'amour*, dried or fresh red-hot chillis, and many other varieties of fruit and vegetable unfamiliar to Western eyes and palates. The meat market and fish market are not for the faint-hearted.

If you are hungry, try some of the snacks available from several stall-holders. Among them you'll find *faratas* (thin pancakes smeared with a hot sauce), *badjahs* (fried pieces of dough), chilli bites and samosas, together with coconut milk and garishly coloured artificial syrups.

The market is open from 06:00 to 18:00 Monday to Saturday, 06:00 to 12:00 on Sunday. If you want to buy perishables, remember that the best quality is to be had

Green Buys

Chou chou – prickly, pear-shaped fruit with a creamy green skin. Bland flavour; can be boiled, fried or stewed, or put in salads and chutney.
Okra/lalo – long green vegetable with ridged sides; buy them small, as mature ones become slimy during cooking.
Manioc – starchy tuber with delicate flavour. Peel, remove stalk then boil and mash, make into croquettes or put in soup. Also pounded into a flour and used to make *biscuits manioc*.
Songes/arouille – edible tuber of elephant ear plant; most kinds are poisonous. Scrub, boil, and peel, serve whole or mash. Use large, purple ones in soups, soufflés or purées, or make into croquettes. Small green ones are best for curries and stews.
Jackfruit – like breadfruit, but can weigh up to 25kg (55lb) Peel skin, discard fibrous core, rinse in vinegar and water to remove milky residue from soft, flaky pulp. Use in chutneys and curries. Large, white seeds resemble chestnuts; young ones roast well.

CHINESE QUARTER

The Chinese Quarter is located in the northern part of the capital. It offers a colourful and lively insight into the Chinese community living on the island. The streets are filled with restaurants selling good Chinese food at affordable prices, as well as a variety of small shops selling anything from traditional clothes to herbal medicines. A free visit can be arranged to one of the oldest printing houses in the country, which publishes the Chinese newspaper, *The Mirror*.

early on while bargains are found towards the end of the day when the vendors want to clear their stalls and are ready to drop their prices. Bargaining is welcomed, and if you don't fall in with this custom you will risk being overcharged. Watch out for pickpockets.

The Chinese Quarter ***

Found just north of Government House and the market, the Chinese Quarter is a hive of activity, with boutiques selling Chinese silks and porcelain, ornamental knick-knacks such as dragons and buddha statues, food and all manner of medicinal herbs. Illuminated by small lanterns, the area by night is much more vibrant than the rest of Port Louis, which is usually very quiet outside office hours.

Paradoxically, the **Jummah Mosque**, the largest on the island, is situated in the Chinese Quarter. On the instructions of the governor, Decaen, land was bought in 1805 for a mosque to meet the religious needs of the immigrant Moslem population. Materials and skilled labour were brought from India, and building started in the

Below left: *Chinatown.*
Below right: *Jummah Mosque, the island's largest.*
Opposite: *A group of Chinese musicians.*

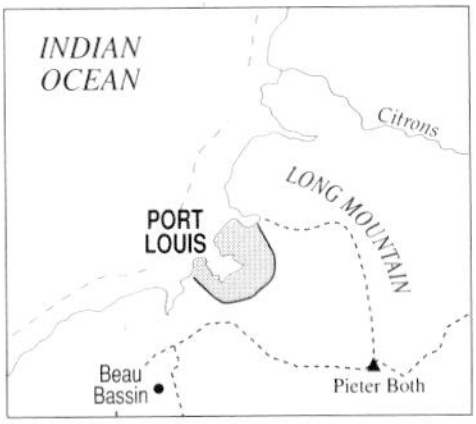

1850s, continuing until 1895. The faithful are still called by the muezzin to pray in its cool interior five times a day. The white plasterwork of the exterior is ornately moulded, and is beautifully offset by dark-green iron railings and wooden shutters. It also features a spired dome, along with heavy, intricately carved wooden doors, inlaid with brass, at the main entrance. Abutting small, rickety shops, the mosque, with its shady courtyards, still ablution pools and quiet prayer rooms, is a peaceful retreat amid the hustle and bustle of the city.

Around Town

While the Place d'Armes can be regarded as the heart and showpiece of Port Louis, the main streets leading off it are important business and shopping areas and also feature some interesting historical buildings.

President John Kennedy St, running parallel to the waterfront, is where you will find **Rogers House** – here a number of embassies, consulates, and airlines are situated, as well as Rogers Travel. Bookings for the **M.V. *Mauritius Pride*** can be done at Island Service Ltd in the building next door. **Victoria Square**, with its bus station and taxi rank conveniently situated for trips to the south, is located just a couple of blocks southwest of Rogers House, between the freeway and **Line Barracks**. The latter, some of whose buildings predate Labourdonnais, now house the police headquarters. **La Chaussée** starts near Line Barracks and runs over the small Pouce Stream and past Company Gardens to Place d'Armes. Passing Mauritours and MTTB on the left, it crosses **Sir William Newton St**, centre of banking and business, and becomes **Royal St**, where one of the best bookshops in Port Louis, Librairie le Trèfle, is found, as well as the attractive entrance to the Jummah Mosque.

Intendance St runs parallel to Sir William Newton St past the other side of Government House; as it reaches

Robert Edward Hart Gardens

Located on the southwest side of the harbour near Fort William, the **Robert Edward Hart Gardens** once had pleasant views of the sea, which are now unfortunately obscured by the sugar terminal. Nevertheless the gardens are still attractive enough in their own right, well maintained, and dotted with the inevitable statues (including one of Lenin). They also house an old **gas factory**, now a national monument and in use, somewhat incongruously, as a sports centre.

Sir Seewoosagur Ramgoolam St it opens out into **Gillet Square**, with the **Municipal Theatre**, designed by French architect, Pierre Poujade, taking pride of place here. This modest theatre, built in 1822 in the neoclassical style, has a beautifully painted ceiling and is said to be the oldest theatre on the Indian Ocean islands. Though it was closed for several years, it has been restored and is now operational again (plays are often performed in Creole). It has contributed a great deal to the culture of the city.

At this point Intendance St becomes **Jules Koenig St** (once named Pope Hennessy St and still known as such by many people and on some maps – a classic example of the confusion that often reigns around the street names in Port Louis!). Further on, the fine, 18th-century **Supreme Court** is on the right.

Just off Jules Koenig St, which eventually runs into the Champ de Mars, are the Catholic and Anglican cathedrals. The Catholic **Cathedral of St Louis**, built in 1932-3, is the third church to stand on this site. The Celtic crosses adorning the towers and pews are the legacy of the Irish Monsignor Leen who was Bishop at the time the cathedral was built. In front of the cathedral is a fountain dating to 1786, and behind is the grand, 19th-century Episcopal Palace. The Anglican **St James Cathedral** on Poudrière St nearby is smaller, simpler, and more solid; some of its walls, several metres thick, date back to French times when a powder magazine existed here. Ward IV, the area between Poudrière St and Signal Mountain, has many fine examples of traditional Mauritian architecture, particularly small, elegant houses. Look out for the wooden presbytery of the **Immaculée Conception** church and the **Hardy-Henry house**, with wrought ironwork on its balconies – both on St Georges St.

Champ de Mars

The Champ de Mars has had a less-than-tranquil past. Its very name, taken from that of the military parade ground in Paris, is a reference to the Roman god of war. The ground in Port Louis was also used as a military parade ground for French, and later British, troops. Volatile sentiment during the French Revolution resulted in the erection of a guillotine on the site, and a goat was sacrificed in order to test the efficacy of its blades. Fortunately, the goat proved to be the only victim. The Champ de Mars was transformed into a race-course in 1812.

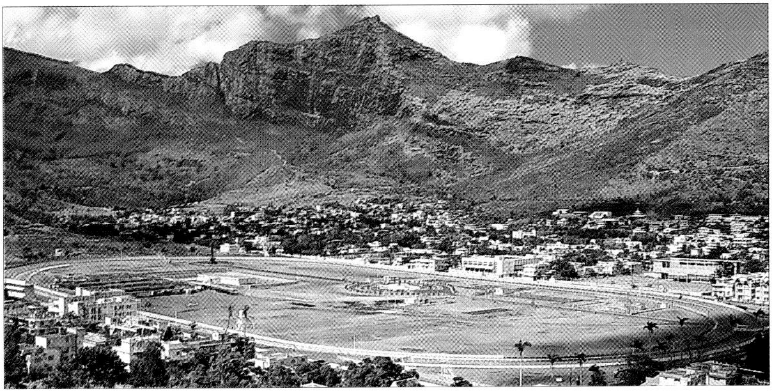

Opposite: *Taking a break: locals and tourists sit on the steps of the main post office, whose architecture dates back to the height of the Victorian era.*
Above: *The Champ de Mars racecourse, set against a backdrop of the Moka Mountains. It is the oldest course in the southern hemisphere.*

Champ de Mars *

Mauritius's only racecourse is the Champ de Mars in Port Louis, home of the **Mauritius Turf Club**. Founded by Colonel Draper in 1812, within a couple of years of the arrival of the British, the club has the distinction of being the second oldest jockey club in the world after its English counterpart. The Champ de Mars was used as a racecourse for the first time in the same year. These days, race meetings are held on Saturdays from May to November. The highlight of the racing calendar is in late August when the Maiden Plate is run over 2600m (2843yd). In the absence of a thoroughbred breeding programme in Mauritius, many of the racehorses are imported from South Africa.

On the north side of the racecourse is the **Lam Soon temple**, one of three Chinese temples in Port Louis. Smoke from sandalwood incense wafts through the gold and red interior of this 19th-century structure, its intricately carved, gold-painted panelling imported from China.

Sainte Croix

Situated in the northeast of the city, the suburb of Ste Croix is famed across the island for the **shrine of Père Laval**, found here near the modern Ste Croix Church. The saint's body lies in a stone sarcophagus surmounted by a plaster-of-Paris effigy. Père Laval, French missionary and doctor, devoted his 23 years on the island to the needs of the sick and poor; to this day he is revered by people of all faiths. Pilgrimages to the shrine are often held, particularly in September, and originate from all over the

Above: *Intricate detail on the domes of the Tamil Kaylasson Temple.*

Fort Adelaide

The gloomy stone fortress overlooking the Champ de Mars was built by the British in 1835-1840. The site was chosen because of its views over the city, the idea being that from the fort the authorities would be alert to any civil unrest. With the abolition of slavery, enforced locally in 1835, this was a very real possibility. Although it is more widely referred to as **La Citadelle**, the Fort took its official name from Queen Adelaide, wife of King William IV. No longer needed as a military post, it is sometimes used as a venue for pop concerts and sound-and-light shows. There are some small handicraft and souvenir shops.

island as well as abroad. Miracle cures, said to have occurred here, are part of the attraction. At the shrine there is a permanent exhibition of his belongings, photographs and letters.

For the sheer exuberance of its ornamentation, the large Tamil **Kaylasson Temple** at nearby **Abercrombie** is worth a visit, or at least a drive past to see the outside. Its enormous domes are a riot of colour, the geometric colonnades at their base covered in moulded abstract designs and figures from Hindu mythology; the building is surrounded by a pink-and-white-striped wall and backed by the beautiful Moka Mountains.

Viewing points **

Two peaks rising high above the town are the steep-sided **Pieter Both** and **le Pouce**, both of which can be climbed if you are fit enough! The latter can be reached through cane fields, but the final part is quite steep; no permission is needed to climb it. For those who get to the top, the rewards are great – a fantastic view of Port Louis and an uninterrupted panorama of the island. To the northwest of le Pouce is the much smaller **Signal Mountain**, a popular viewing point of the city, and one of the citizens' favourite places for walks in the cool of evening. A signalling post in years gone by, it has followed modern communication trends and is now surmounted by a radio and television transmitter. Another excellent spot from which to view the capital is **Fort Adelaide**; situated on a spur of the surrounding mountains, it is one of four forts built by the British in the environs of Port Louis.

Shopping and Art Galleries

The Caudan Waterfront has dozens of quality shops, which are perfect for browsing. Otherwise the following shops sell items likely to appeal to the tourist. National Handicraft Centre, opposite the Company Gardens at 10 Edith Cavell St, and La Maison de l'Artisanat, on La Chaussée, sell quality **handicrafts**. Duty-free **jewellery** can be purchased from Mikado, Sir William Newton St, Poncini, 2 Jules Koenig St (opposite the theatre), Bijouchic, 15 La Chaussée, or Bijouterie Bienvenue, 61 Lord Kitchener St, while **clothing** with a local flavour is obtainable from Bongo or The Spot, both on Royal St, among others. In addition to clothing, Planet on La Chaussée sells a variety of craftwork and quality souvenirs. For **flowers**, visit Anthuriums and Orchids, Intendance St, and Fleurs des Tropiques, 35 Sir William Newton St. Good **bookshops** are Amicale and Le Trèfle on Royal St or Corner House, corner of Royal and Bourbon St.

Port Louis Art Gallery, located on Mallefille St, exhibits the work of local artists, with a new exhibition each month. It is open 09:00-16:00 Monday to Friday, and 09:00-12:00 on Saturday. **Galerie Hélène de Senneville** has a branch in Belmont House, Vieux Conseil St, tel: 212-8339.

Domaine les Pailles

In some ways, Domaine les Pailles, an estate occupying some 6600ha (16,310 acres) of land, seems to be trying to provide some relief from the effects of development, by holding on to some of the island's history which is often overlooked for the sake of progress, and catering to the recreational needs of an increasingly developed and industrialized society. In addition to having historical appeal, the estate aims to attract nature lovers, gamblers, gourmets and horse-riders, drawing together many of the best of Mauritian traditions.

Below: *The gates to the Domaine les Pailles estate, with the stately casino building behind.*

Above: *Alambic distillery, still used to make rum at Domaine les Pailles.*

Visitors can explore the countryside in a black lacquered horse-drawn carriage or a four-wheel-drive vehicle that can cope with rougher terrain. Drives offer splendid views of the western plains and take up to two hours. If you can ride, explore the countryside on horseback – there are 42 horses stabled here. Two trained instructors are on hand to accompany treks in the scenic foothills of the Moka mountain range, or to give lessons. Welsh ponies are available for smaller children.

A carefully tended **spice garden** contains exotic spice plants from Asia and America, while the **mill**, a copy of the first sugar mill in French-ruled Mauritius, shows the process of sugar production as it would have been in 1770. An ox-drawn cart brings the sugar cane from the estate's plantation, and the mill, also powered by oxen, crushes the cane. Open vats collect the juice from the crushed cane which turns into syrup, some of which is distilled into rum in the **Alambic distillery** alongside the mill. The Alambic is a faithful replica of a model, dating back to 1758.

A number of very rare Mauritius kestrels that were bred in captivity at the Black River Aviary have now been released in the Domaine. These are sometimes seen from walks along the narrow mountain paths in the wooded gorges. Deer, hares and monkeys can also be glimpsed in the undergrowth. Visitors walking or driving through the grounds are bound to come across royal ferns and ancient ebony trees, several centuries old.

Children over five can visit the **Children's Corner**, whose entertainment programme includes pony rides. Gamblers can try their luck at the **Casino du Domaine**, while **mini-golf** is also an activity that is available. On Friday nights Domaine les Pailles plays host to local musicians.

Fine Food at Domaine les Pailles

Domaine les Pailles has five restaurants, aimed at satisfying a variety of tastes. The most elegant is **Fouquet's**, after its namesake in Paris. Resembling an old manor house of early colonial days, decked out in Indian marble and Malagasy rosewood, and furnished with period pieces. It is also the most interesting architecturally. The best French cuisine combines with elegant decor to please even the most sophisticated diner. **La Cannelle Rouge** provides snacks and meals as well as more substantial fare in the Creole tradition, with the same guarantee of quality. **Fu Xiao** and **The Indra** feature Chinese and Indian dishes respectively, with the Pailles restaurants' usual attention to detail not lacking. For those who long for something really Western, there is the pizzeria, the **Dolce Vita**.

Five restaurants provide a range of top-quality food. As yet the only formal accommodation is The Lodge; set on the mountain shoulder and offering superb views, the cosy cottages are designed for small groups. Overnight camping can also be arranged for those who like to sleep under the stars.

Le Domaine les Pailles is open Monday to Saturday, 09:30 to 17:00. Other opening hours, night safaris and evening meals can be arranged with management. The Domaine is just off the highway to the south of Port Louis, about ten minutes' drive from the city.

Sir Seewoosagur Ramgoolam Botanic Garden

Formerly called the Royal Botanic Gardens, the Sir Seewoosagur Ramgoolam Botanic Garden is still known simply as **Pamplemousses** by most people. The 24ha (60-acre) site, 11km (7 miles) outside Port Louis, was originally purchased by Bertrand Mahé de Labourdonnais in 1735 as part of a country residence (the original chateau of Mon Plaisir) whose land was to be cultivated as a supply garden for the ships calling at the harbour. But the man to whom the gardens owe their rightful place in history was Pierre Poivre, the French Intendant of Mauritius and keen horticulturalist who took charge of the gardens in the latter part of the 18th century, and landscaped them in their present form with

Peter Piper

Famous in the English-speaking world for his 'peck of pickled peppers', **Pierre Poivre** lived up to his name and enthusiastically imported spices from the East to plant in Mauritius. In the hope that they would make the island's fortune, various spices were cultivated, especially cloves and nutmeg, but unfortunately for the early colonists, and contrary to expectations, these plants did not flourish in Mauritius.

'Piper' is the Latin word from which the modern English 'pepper' was derived.

Below: *The renowned pond of giant* Victoria amazonica *water lilies in the Sir Seewoosagur Ramgoolam Botanic Garden at Pamplemousses.*

What's in a Name?

Some of the trees in the Pamplemousses Gardens have rather peculiar names.

The orange-like berry of the **marmalade box tree** is made into marmalade as well as a preserve known as 'genipap', while the **chewing gum tree** or chicle tree provides the gum used for making natural chewing gum. The bark, twigs and leaves of the **fish poison tree**, when thrown into the water, will stun or intoxicate fish, making them easy to catch.

Various palms have also gained curious names – the **hurricane palm** because of its ability to withstand cyclones, the **wine palm** because its juice when fermented is enjoyed as a drink, especially in India. The **sugar palm** also produces a sap which can be made into an alcoholic drink, although it can also be dried until it has a crystalline texture, when it becomes a bit like toffee.

a variety of features including shady avenues, ponds and terraces. Today the gardens are most famous for their giant *Victoria amazonica* water lilies whose huge leaves will reputedly withstand a weight of up to 45 kg (100 lb). The flowers open in the afternoon and close in the morning; they are white on the first day of blossoming, but turn pink by the second day.

More notable for its trees than for floral displays, Pamplemousses boasts over 60 varieties of palm, 24 of which are indigenous to the Mascarene islands. One of these is the talipot palm, known in India as the '100-year tree', which flowers once after about 50 years then dies. Ebony and mahogany trees also thrive in the gardens.

The original chateau of **Mon Plaisir** is no longer in existence; the present house of the same name was constructed in about 1850 in a different position, from where there are pleasant views of Pieter Both and the Moka mountain range. Plans are afoot to refurbish and develop it. There is also a reconstruction of an early sugar mill, as well as a monument (actually the base of an old statue) described as the tomb of the ill-fated Paul and Virginie. Other items of interest are the small deer park and the giant Aldabra tortoises from Seychelles, where they are an endangered species. The main entrance to the gardens is worth noting; created in France, the beautiful wrought-iron gates were donated to the gardens by François Liénard de la Mivoie, and having won a prize at the International Exhibition at the Crystal Palace, London, in 1862, were installed six years later.

Below: *The Liénard Obelisk in the Botanic Garden.*

Official guides offer their services in exchange for a tip, thus avoiding the hassle of dealing with dubious characters offering to take you around. A guidebook by the Conservator of Forests can be bought at the gardens, which are open from 07:00 to 17:00 in winter and 07:00 to 18:00 in summer. There is no admission charge.

Port Louis and Surrounds at a Glance

Best Times to Visit

Any time but summer, when the city can be oppressively hot and sticky, and there are sudden downpours.

Getting There

From the **north** it is up to ½ hour's **drive**, travelling mainly on the new highway. From the **east** or **west coasts**, allow ¾ hour; from the **south**, 1-1½ hours. **Domaine les Pailles** and **Pamplemousses** are 10-15 minutes away.
The main **bus** terminuses are Victoria Square near the docks and Immigration Square near the market. Allow extra time for bus travel.

Getting Around

It is fairly easy to get about **on foot**. With a regular street grid and mountains for orientation, you are unlikely to get lost.
If you **drive**, get 'pay and display' coupons at petrol stations or Mauritius Telecom offices; there are no parking meters.
A convenient alternative is to hire a **taxi** for the day; the driver can wait for you, or take you on a drive-tour of the city.

Where to Stay

Hotels are mainly for business travellers although increasingly geared to tourists.
Labourdonnais Waterfront Hotel, in the heart of Le Caudan, first-class facilities; tel: 202-4000, fax: 202-4040.
St Georges Hotel, St Georges St, is one of the better establishments here; tel: 211-2581.

Where to Eat

Port Louis
La Bonne Marmite, 18 Sir William Newton St, elegant venue, one of the best in Port Louis; gourmet restaurant upstairs with local and Indian specialities, café and pub on ground floor; tel: 212-2403.
Le Carri Poulé, Place d'Armes, excellent reputation for interesting, authentic Indian/Creole food; buffet Wednesday-Friday, evening meals Friday and Saturday; tel: 212-1295.
Keg and Marlin, Les Docks Building, Caudan Waterfront. Trendy English-style pub offering great meals and snacks. Open till late; tel: 211-6821.
Lai Min, peaceful retreat in the heart of the Chinese Quarter; excellent food, interesting decor; open evenings and weekends; tel: 242-0042.
La Palmeraie, Sir Celicourt Antelme St, good French cuisine, courtyard setting; also serves light meals; weekday lunches only; tel: 212-2597.
DSL Coffee Shop, Cathedral Square; typical South Indian vegetarian food; tel: 212-0259.
Grand Rivière Nord-Ouest
Tung Fong, good Chinese eatery set around an enchanting courtyard; tel: 208-6279.

Domaine les Pailles
see p. 106; tel: 212-4225.

Activities and Excursions

The Mauritius Institute, open Monday, Tuesday, Thursday, Friday 09:00-16:00, Saturday 09:00-12:00. Admission free. tel: 212-0639.
Pamplemousses Gardens and **Domaine les Pailles** (tel: 212-4225) are often included in package tours; public buses to the gardens leave from the Labourdonnais terminus.

Useful Contacts

Mauritius Tourism Promotion Authority, 11th floor, Air Mauritius Centre, John Kennedy St, Port Louis; tel: 208-6397, fax: 212-5142.
Mauritius Travel and Tourist Bureau, Royal St, tel: 208-2041/2, fax: 208-8607.
Mauritours, 10 Sir William Newton St, tel: 212-1260, fax: 212-4465.
Concorde Travel Agent and Tour Operator, La Chaussée, tel: 212-6002, fax: 212-2585.

PORT LOUIS	J	F	M	A	M	J	J	A	S	O	N	D
AVERAGE TEMP. °F	82	82	81	81	77	73	73	73	73	75	79	81
AVERAGE TEMP. °C	28	28	27	27	25	23	23	23	23	24	26	27
Hours of Sun Daily	8	8	7	7	7	7	7	7	8	8	9	9
SEA TEMP. °F	82	80	82	80	78	77	75	73	73	75	79	80
SEA TEMP. °C	28	27	28	27	26	25	24	23	23	24	26	27
RAINFALL in	7	7	4	3	2	1	1	1	1	4	1	4
RAINFALL mm	165	183	91	87	41	24	20	24	31	18	33	91
Days of Rainfall	8	6	8	7	4	4	3	5	4	3	2	6
Humidity	75	78	74	78	68	65	71	62	62	61	68	71

7
The Central Plateau

During the malaria and cholera epidemics which struck the coastal areas in the 1860s, people fled en masse to the cooler central plateau, and the small, isolated villages there expanded rapidly. The towns of **Beau Bassin/Rose Hill**, **Quatre Bornes**, **Phoenix/Vacoas** and **Curepipe** have grown considerably in the last 130 years and now form an almost continuous strip of urban development, dormitory areas for the capital's commuters. The district of Plaines Wilhems, where these towns lie, is home to about a third of the population, making it the most densely populated region. Northeast of it lies the district of Moka; devoted largely to agriculture, most of it is seldom visited by tourists.

For many visitors the plateau is the least attractive part of the island, but the roads have now been resurfaced and the government has made a concerted effort to clean up and promote the area, making it a more pleasant place which, it is hoped, will draw visitors. The urban sprawl, however, gives way to plantations in the east and is edged in the west and north by some of the island's highest mountains, dotted with reservoirs, all of which alleviate the drabness of the built-up landscape; there are also reminders of the island's more gracious past in some lovely colonial mansions.

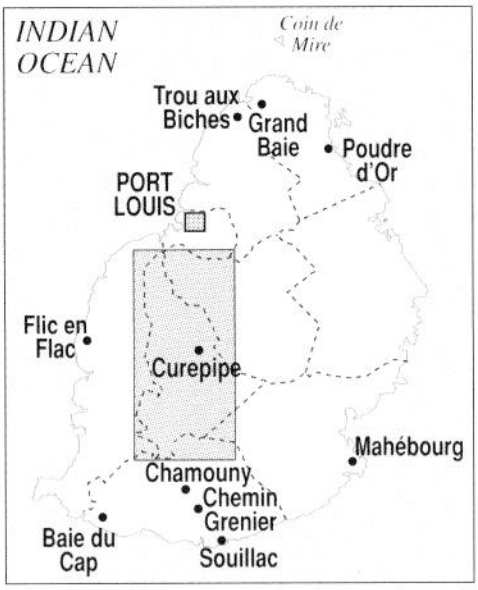

CLIMATE

The residential areas of the plateau have a much **cooler** and **wetter** climate than the coastal belt. Curepipe has a high rainfall the year round, and is often topped by a cloudy sky: when in Curepipe, always be prepared with an umbrella and, depending on the time of year, some warm clothing. The lower-lying neighbouring areas of Quatre Bornes and Beau Bassin/Rose Hill nearby share the cooler climes of Curepipe, although they are not as wet.

Opposite: *From a view-point above Henrietta.*

CUREPIPE

Curepipe is located halfway between Port Louis and the airport at Plaisance, 21km (13 miles) either way, and at 550m (1800ft) it is the highest settlement on the island.

> **DON'T MISS**
>
> *** a walk to the lovely Tamarind Falls
> *** a visit to Eurêka
> ** Trou aux Cerfs, Curepipe
> ** shopping in Curepipe and Quatre Bornes, and at Phoenix's Continent shopping centre
> * hiking up the Corps de Garde mountain
> * the Plaza Theatre complex at Rose Hill

Its climate is temperate, and it is sometimes described as having two seasons: the season of rains and the rainy season! Prepared for all eventualities, local residents protect themselves from sun and rain alike with umbrellas.

The area was once covered by thick forest that hid deer and runaway slaves, but as the forest was cleared to make way for sugar cane, it became easier and safer to settle in the interior. Like the other plateau towns, Curepipe grew suddenly with the influx of people from the coast in the 1860s; in 1866, the Port Louis-Mahébourg railway line was built, making it much more accessible, too. It now has a population nearing 100,000.

Curepipe lacks charm and atmosphere, but the town and its green surrounds do make a change from the sea; you could even forget that you're in the middle of a tropical island, with the beaches not far away. Driving through the tiny streets, some unnamed, some with two names, you catch glimpses, between the bamboo hedges, of renovated colonial houses with steeply pitched roofs and large verandahs, in marked contrast to the modern proliferation of ugly concrete structures. Floréal is an exclusive suburb on a ridge on the northwest side of town; looking out to the distant west coast, it is favoured by executives and diplomats.

The **Curepipe Botanical Gardens** are smaller and more informal than those at Pamplemousses. Water features, lawns, and indigenous shrubs are in sharp contrast to the concrete environment of downtown Curepipe. The office of the Conservator of

> **DODO CLUB**
>
> The Franco-Mauritian answer to the English Gymkhana Club at Vacoas was the **Dodo Club** at Curepipe, which soon became a focal point of Franco-Mauritian society, the highlight of the social calendar being the New Year's Eve ball. These days it is notable as a private sports club, with football and rugby being particularly popular; there is also a nine-hole golf course. Membership is still exclusively white, unusual in what is otherwise a reasonably racially harmonious society.

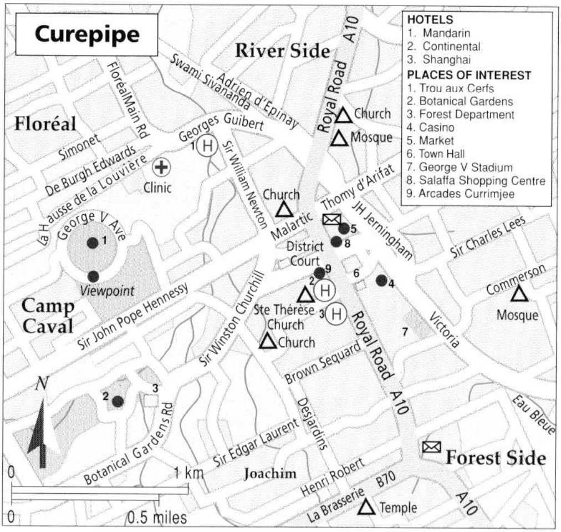

Above: *The dome and tower of the Ste Hélène Basilica in Curepipe.*

Forests, from whom permission is needed to visit many of the island's nature reserves, is situated here.

The town hall, found on Elizabeth Ave, is a pleasing building which has been under renovation for some time. Interestingly, it was originally a fine colonial house in Moka, until 1902 when it was dismantled and re-assembled in Curepipe. In the garden stands a bronze statue of Paul and Virginie by the well-known local sculptor, Prosper d'Epinay.

Gambling

The **Casino de Maurice** on Teste de Buch Rd is a casino in the European style. Visitors are allowed free entrance, and you do not need to present your passport in order to gamble. Open 21:00-03:00; tel: 675-5021.

Shopping **

Mauritius is a duty-free shopping destination, and indeed shopping is one of the main attractions of Curepipe (although it is now rivalled by the new shopping centres at Quatre Bornes and Phoenix). The **Salaffa Shopping Centre** and **Arcades Currimjee** both sell interesting products; Chinese silks and clothing can be bought at City of Peking and jewellery at Mikado in Salaffa Centre, or try Beautés de Chine in Arcades Currimjee for a wide range of Chinese products. Booklovers will enjoy the Librairie du Trèfle and the Librairie Allot in Arcades Currimjee.

Several shops in **Forest Side** specialize in wooden model ships, namely Comajora and Juratone in Brasserie Rd, Voiliers de l'Océan in Celicourt Antelme Rd and La Marine en Bois in Gustave-Colin Rd. Nearer the city centre, La Serenissima and Le Chandelier, both on Royal Rd, also stock model boats. Models of Creole and colonial houses, an offshoot of the model ship industry, are sold at Maquettes de Maisons Traditionelles Mauriciennes in Forest Side.

Floréal is home to duty-free enterprises selling model ships and diamonds. Imported from South Africa, diamonds are cut, polished and re-exported under EPZ regulations. They must be bought at least two days before departure, and are sealed and put in a safe until you leave; they are then delivered to you at the airport. If you intend to buy diamonds from the duty-free shops, remember to bring your passport, air ticket and foreign currency (notes, credit cards or traveller's cheques).

The **Prisunic supermarket**, situated nearly opposite the Town Hall, was until recently the largest supermarket in Mauritius, and is still a good place to go for speciality foods and drinks, wines and cheeses, many of which are imported, as well as a host of everyday requirements. **Sik Yuen Supermarket** also has a wide variety of stock.

Remember that, although regular shopping hours are generally 9:00-18:00 or 08:30-19:30, Thursday is early closing day, so don't expect to do any shopping after midday. Many shops are closed all day on Sunday.

Model Ships

About 30 years ago a Mauritian with a passion for model ships hired a couple of craftsmen to help produce and sell these unusual souvenirs. Others copied him and the craft is now widely practised on a commercial basis.

The model ships, or *maquettes*, can take about 400 hours to make. Attention is paid to tiny details, to ensure that the boats are of a high enough quality to grace the most elegant study or living room. Be wary of boats made up from kits imported from Asia. Look closely at detailed work and check that nothing has been made of plastic.

Models are usually securely packed, and as most are not more than 80cm (31in) long, they may often be carried as hand luggage. If not, be prepared to pay freightage costs.

Trou aux Cerfs **

The crater of an extinct volcano, **Trou aux Cerfs** is 85m (279ft) deep and over 200m (656ft) in diameter. These days it is Curepipe's main attraction, with a panoramic view of the island from the top of the crater: Montagne du Rempart, les Trois Mamelles, and le Corps de Garde, as well as the distant west coast, can all be seen. You can also climb down the sides of the crater which are clad in dense forest; at the bottom is a small lake. Volcanologists say that the crater is probably linked with the volcanoes on Réunion, and as long as the volcanoes there are active, volcanic activity on Mauritius is unlikely to occur. But should the activity on Réunion cease, pressure could build up under Mauritius, and volcanoes long dormant could erupt again. Ever optimistic, entrepreneurial Mauritians have nevertheless suggested building an amphitheatre in the crater.

Opposite: *Vegetable stalls under colourful awnings at the Curepipe market.*
Left: *Curepipe has grown up around the volcanic crater of Trou aux Cerfs. It is possible to walk down the inside of the crater to a small lake at the bottom.*

The Small Plateau Towns

Beau Bassin/Rose Hill

Situated midway between Curepipe and Port Louis, these two towns merged soon after they were established, and have belonged to the same municipality since 1896.

The rather sleepy town of Beau Bassin is home to a teachers' training college, police training school, prison, and mental hospital; it has some redeeming features too, such as the attractive **Sacré Coeur Church**, built in the 1880s, and the **Balfour Gardens** overlooking the Sorèze Falls on the Plaines Wilhems River to the distant Moka Mountains. Near the gardens is a gracious white mansion, **Le Thabor**, which is now a retreat for clergy from the diocese of Port Louis. Originally the home of a British army captain, La Tour Blanche, as this house was once called, was the gathering place for British high society. Its guests have included Charles Darwin in 1836 and Pope John Paul II in 1989.

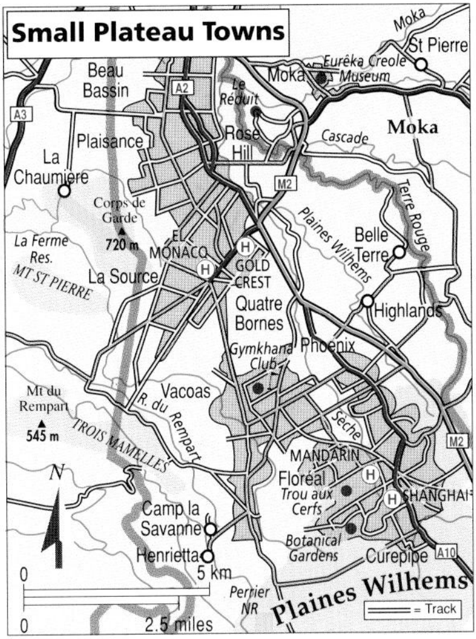

The more lively Rose Hill has long been the cultural centre of Mauritius, and today it is the home of the **British Council**, the **Centre Charles Baudelaire**, (a French cultural centre which stages art exhibitions and theatrical performances and also has an important library), and the **Plaza Theatre**. The latter is the largest theatre complex on the Indian Ocean islands; plays are performed here in all the main languages, and operas and concerts are regularly held. The Plaza complex also houses a theatre museum, library

and the Max Boullé Art Gallery, which exhibits local artists' work. The grand Victorian building near the central bus terminus, once the city's railway station and now the post office, is in refreshing contrast with the soulless modern architecture surrounding it. Also harking back to the past is the Rose Hill Pharmacy on Royal Rd, decked out in the style of a 19th-century apothecary (it does, however, sell modern medicines as well as jars of various preparations!).

MOUNTAIN WALKS

The **Corps de Garde** can be reached fairly easily from Rose Hill, and makes a pleasant walk with spectacular views of both the plateau and, overlooking La Ferme reservoir nestling at its foot, the west coast. If you would like to join an organized group, contact the **Centre d'Excursion de Beau Bassin**, a private walking group, or the government-run **Randonnée du Coeur**.

Rose Hill has become a commercial centre with the modern Galeries Evershine and other shopping centres as well as many small shops in town. On the whole, though, the shops here are not like the upmarket boutiques in Grand Baie, and a more interesting diversion could be watching the hawkers drive a hard bargain at the roadside. Souvenir-hunters can go to Auction Mart on Royal Rd, or Craft Aid in Edgar Laurent Rd which employs disabled people. For books on Mauritius, try Librairie le Cygne in the Magic Lantern complex or Editions de l'Océan Indien in the west of town on Vandermeersch St.

Quatre Bornes

The name of Quatre Bornes refers to the four boundaries formed by the sugar plantations in the area. The town is situated between Candos Hill in the southeast and le Corps de Garde on its western side; a Hindu temple can be seen perched on the slopes of the mountain.

The new **Orchard Shopping Centre**, a huge, attractive complex, has now livened up the shopping scene, and for clothing, fabric and knick-knacks the foire or open-air market at Quatre Bornes is reputed to be the best on the island. Bargain-hunters will like the cheap, famous-name 'seconds' from the EPZ factories. For souvenirs don't miss SPES (Societé des Petites Entreprises Spécialisées, where disabled people make a wide range of craftware) or Bricolage Mauricien, both on Labourdonnais St, and the shop of the Mauritius Alliance of Women in St Jean Rd.

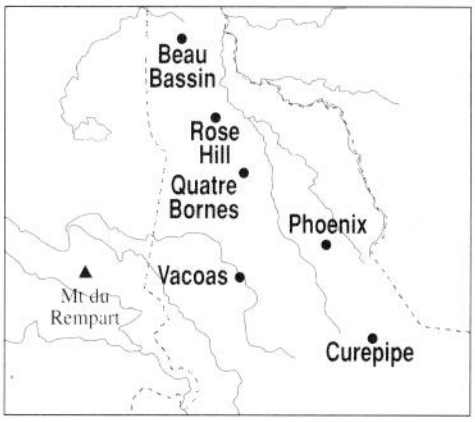

Opposite: *The Plaza Theatre Complex at Rose Hill.*
Left: *The main highway across the central plateau, running through Curepipe, Quatre Bornes, and on towards Port Louis.*

Vacoas/Phoenix

The twin towns of Vacoas and Phoenix have a temperate climate (said to be the best on the island) in which gardens flourish. During British rule, this is where civil servants tended to live; their social life revolved around the **Gymkhana Club**, which opened its doors in 1844 as a polo club. Today it has an 18-hole golf course, swimming pool, snooker room and clubhouse. Visitors can take out temporary membership if they wish to play golf here. British naval communications and meteorological communication were once based in Vacoas; nowadays it is the headquarters of the Special Military Force – equivalent to the army – as well as being the seat of the Anglican bishop.

Vacoas forms one municipality with Phoenix, which is primarily an industrial area. The famous Phoenix beer and other beverages are produced here. Keen shoppers may be interested in exploring the huge Continent shopping centre, which boasts an international-standard hypermarket, over 30 boutiques and a 'Food Court'. Ceuneau House on Royal Rd where model ships are made, and the Phoenix Factory Shop near the brewery for cheap famous-name clothing, will also interest shoppers.

MARINE CONSERVATION

Founded in 1964, the **Mauritius Underwater Group** (MUG) is affiliated to the British Sub Aqua Club, and welcomes contact with visiting underwater enthusiasts. Tuesdays are open club nights. On the same premises on Station Rd, Vacoas, is the **Marine Conservation Society**, set up recently to stimulate public awareness of the island's rich marine environment and the damage being done to it. Slide shows and lectures are presented, and marine surveys carried out; artificial reefs have been created by sinking old boats, and they are now looking into establishing marine parks. Tel: 696-5368.

Colonial Houses

Le Réduit

The official residence of the president of Mauritius, Le Réduit, is situated near Moka at the confluence of two tributaries of the Grande Rivière Nord-Ouest. The original part of the building was built in 1748 by the French Governor, David, on a bluff between the two rivers. Initially it was intended as a refuge for the island's women and children, to be used in the event of invasion by foreign forces. Enlarged and improved on as time passed, this gracious colonial house became first unofficially and later officially the residence of the French and British governors of the colony, and, since the country was declared a republic in 1992, the president. The building eventually became a hybrid of French and Victorian architecture as new wings, terraces, colonnades and verandahs were added, and stone replaced wood in response to the ravages of cyclones. The 132ha (325-acre) grounds were originally laid out by a French landscape gardener but later submitted to English influence, appropriate to its riverside setting. The house is closed to the public except for two occasions each year (in March and October), when one is permitted to stroll around the pleasant gardens.

'Eureka!'

Legend has it that the Creole house's intriguing name came about when Leclézio, one of its early owners, exclaimed in excitement at bidding successfully for the property at an auction. It remained in his family until it was opened as a museum in 1986.

Eurêka ***

Not far from Le Réduit, in the picturesque town of **Moka** on the other side of the freeway, lies an old Creole-style house known as Eurêka. This attractive house, set in a 47ha (117-acre) tropical garden with superb views across a ravine, was built in 1830.

Reputed to be the largest house on the island, it has 109 doors and windows, attesting to the need for cool breezes during the hot summer. The house, which in the past hosted members of the British royal family, is still furnished with fine period furniture. The upstairs area, once set aside for the first proprietor's 17 children, is now an art gallery, with a permanent exhibition of old photographs, maps and models of traditional Mauritian houses.

Left: *The wooden, Creole-style house of Eurêka lies in tranquil surrounds.*

The cottages in the courtyard around the back of the house were once servants' quarters and now house curio shops. Tea is served on the wide verandah of the main house, as are Creole meals if you book in advance. The house is open every day from 09:30 to 17:00; tel: 433-4951. Free guided tours are available.

For a pleasant drive in the area, take the road along the southern side of the Moka Range and through Malenga, past le Pouce and the Pieter Both mountains.

Above: *At the back of Eurêka are several cottages, such as this one, which were formerly servants' quarters.*

Lakes and Reservoirs

Around Curepipe, especially to the south and southwest, lie several lakes and reservoirs. Popular among the residents of the plateau as places to drive, walk or picnic, they are peaceful, scenic places to get away from it all.

Mare aux Vacoas

The closest and by far the largest of these bodies of water is the large reservoir known as Mare aux Vacoas, which is the main water supply of the plateau towns. Mare aux Vacoas is almost entirely surrounded by a forest of *vacoas* or pandanus trees, said to be rich in deer life; from near here, there are wonderful views over the Black River Gorges to the sea in the west.

Tamarind Falls and Mare Longue Reservoir ***

The Tamarind Falls are the highest in Mauritius, cascading 295m (968ft) from the **Tamarind Falls Reservoir** in a series of seven falls and finally dropping into a deep gorge, where it is possible to swim. They can be reached by road from Vacoas, although permission to use this road must be obtained in Curepipe from the Central Electricity Board which has hydroelectric power stations here. Alternatively follow the small road down from **Le Pétrin** junction which leads to the breathtakingly beautiful Black River Gorges; a further track off to the right of this

Wild Guavas

The ***goyave de Chine***, a kind of wild guava, grows in abundance in the Mare aux Vacoas, Grand Bassin and Black River Gorges area. The fruit ripen between March and July, and Mauritians organize guava-picking expeditions. When very ripe, the small guava tastes like a slightly acidic strawberry; while the island's neighbours from Réunion pick them at this stage, Mauritians prefer them slightly more acidic and harvest them before full maturity.

Kanaka Crater

Not far from Grand Bassin is **Kanaka Crater**, an extinct volcanic crater. Surrounded by indigenous forest and undergrowth, it is home to a variety of local birds. A pleasant few hours' walk, starting near Bois Chéri, meanders along tracks through a tea plantation to the crater.

Shiva

According to Hindu doctrine, the godhead is split into three deities: Brahma the creator, Vishnu the preserver, and Shiva the destroyer. Shiva is the most popular of them; he is also known as Gangadhara, 'the one who carries the Ganges', and from his head the Ganges is said to issue. Many Hindu temples have a *shiva lingam*, a sacred stone which represents the first manifestation of Shiva and holds this god's energy.

can be taken to the **Mare Longue Reservoir** and the Tamarind Falls. A number of viewpoints allow the walker to take in spectacular views towards the coast. Wear good walking shoes and only tackle the paths if you are reasonably fit as they can be demanding in places. The bus stop nearest to the falls is at Henrietta. A map showing the walking trails in the area is displayed on a board at Le Pétrin.

Grand Bassin

Situated in the Savanne district, almost directly south of the Mare aux Vacoas, is Grand Bassin, a crater lake whose banks, formed out of basalt and lava, reach a height of 702m (2303ft). In the midst of the deep, tranquil lake is a small island.

Grand Bassin was originally a favourite hunting ground for the early settlers but later it grew in importance as a central part of Indo-Mauritian folk culture. Grand Bassin is a sacred place of pilgrimage for hundreds of thousands of Hindus who, ever since the first pilgrimage took place in 1897, have come to pray to the deity Shiva on its banks each February on the occasion of Maha Shivaratree. Temples, shrines and sanctuaries were built on its banks, and Maha Shivaratree has become the largest Hindu festival outside India. In 1972, water from the Ganges River was poured ceremonially into the lake, and since then the lake has been known among the island's Hindus as **'Ganga Talao'**; popular mythology has it that they are also linked by underground springs. Holy water is collected in small containers and carried back to home shrines to be poured on the *shiva lingam*. Worshippers also float small lights on banana leaves on the lake to symbolize similar offerings of floating flowers placed in the Ganges.

The lakeside setting is dominated by a temple which visitors may enter provided they remove their shoes and are decently clad.

Below: *Hindu pilgrims on the shores of Grand Bassin.*

The Central Plateau at a Glance

Best Times to Visit

Temperatures are always **cooler** on the plateau, however, the chances of **rain** are much greater than at the coast, especially in **summer**, so take a raincoat or umbrella. If you are in Mauritius in **March** or **October**, find out from the MGTO whether **Le Réduit** will be open during your stay.

Getting There

The **highway** runs across the centre of the island, so access from Port Louis, the north and the southeast is very easy. From the east coast you will probably pass through **Quartier Militaire**, while several small roads lead from the west coast resorts. The road through **Plaine Champagne** is particularly scenic. Give yourself ½-1 hour from most points on the coast. **Buses** link the plateau towns with Port Louis, Mahébourg, and a few coastal resorts.

Getting Around

Hiring a **taxi** for the day can be more useful than hiring a car: drivers should be familiar with the main places of interest; they also know the roads where signposts let you down. Otherwise, **buses** run reasonably regularly between these towns, and distances within them are easily walkable.

Where to Stay

This area's hotels are aimed at the short-stay business visitor; unlike Port Louis, though, there are a few quality hotels here, although standards are not as high as at the resort hotels.

Curepipe
L'Auberge du Petit Cerf, 23 Anderson St, old house with charming garden; communal facilities; tel: 676-2892.

Quatre Bornes
Gold Crest Hotel, rated as Mauritius' best business class hotel, tel: 454-5945, fax: 454-9599.
El Monaco Hotel, 17 Saint Jean Rd, garden setting; tel: 425-2631, fax: 425-1072.
The Garden House, Stanley Ave, pleasant, quality guesthouse; excursions arranged; tel/fax: 424-1214.
Auberge de Rose Hill, 275 Royal Rd, basic but pleasant; tel: 464-1793.

Where to Eat

Curepipe
Golden Lion, Sir Winston Churchill St, Chinese fare and seafood; tel: 676-1965.
La Nouvelle Potinière, smart, popular lunch venue; mouth-watering French food with a Creole influence; tel: 676-2648.
Le Pot de Terre, lunchtime snacks, coffee and cake from early morning to late afternoon; tel: 676-2204.

Rose Hill
New Magic Lantern, Chinese restaurant with karaoke; tel: 464-2444.

Quatre Bornes
Rolly's Steak and Seafood, St Jean Rd, European-style steakhouse; tel: 454-8998.
Piment Rouge, for spicy Creole and Indian cuisine; tel: 464-4444.
Happy Valley, authentic Chinese food, good service; tel: 454-6065.
Café Dragon Vert, La Louise; great Chinese food, local and European cuisine; tel: 424-4564.
Tannur, St Jean Rd, excellent Indian fare, no alcohol served; tel: 465-0856.

Phoenix
La Belle Epoque, Sayed Hossen Avenue, Phoenix, tel: 697-1386.

Activities and Excursions

Centre d'Excursion de Beau Bassin, tel: 454-0505, organizes walking trips.

Gamblers can visit Curepipe's **Casino de Maurice**.

CUREPIPE	J	F	M	A	M	J	J	A	S	O	N	D
AVERAGE TEMP. °F	75	79	79	77	73	72	70	70	70	73	75	77
AVERAGE TEMP. °C	24	26	26	25	23	22	21	21	21	23	24	25
Hours of Sun Daily	8	8	7	6	6	6	6	6	7	7	8	8
RAINFALL in	13	13	12	11	8	7	8	6	5	4	5	11
RAINFALL mm	328	322	309	292	244	175	194	160	114	104	138	286
Days of Rainfall	16	16	17	17	14	14	14	14	10	11	9	13
Humidity	82	84	84	83	81	79	78	78	78	78	79	81

Travel Tips

Tourist Information

The official source of tourist information is the **Mauritius Tourism Promotion Authority,** Air Mauritius Centre, John Kennedy St, Port Louis (tel: 208-6397, fax: 212-5142). They also have an information counter at the airport (tel: 637-6397) and offices in New York and London. Alternatively, try **Air Mauritius**, which promotes tourism as well as arranging flights. In Australia, try the **Mauritius Tourist Information Bureau** in Perth.

The main tour operators include the following:

Mauritours, arranges accommodation, transfers and excursions; head office, Rose Hill (tel: 454-1666,fax: 454-1682), branches in Port Louis, Quatre Bornes and Grand Baie, representatives at all large hotels.

Mauritius Travel and Tourist Bureau, Curepipe (tel: 208-2041), also in Port Louis and at the airport.

Concorde Travel and Tours, head office on La Chaussée, Port Louis (tel: 208-5041, fax 212-2585); branches in Curepipe and at the airport.

White Sand Travel and Tours, head office on La Chaussée, Port Louis (tel: 212-6092).

Entry Requirements

You must hold a valid passport and a return or onward ticket, and may not be gainfully employed in Mauritius.

Nationals of most European and Commonwealth countries do not require visas. If necessary, a visitor's visa is normally granted for three months and can be renewed for three months. Visas can be obtained from Mauritian embassies and high commissions; otherwise ask your travel agent to put you in touch with the nearest government representative.

An entry form must be filled in by each passport holder on arrival, stating the address where you will be staying in Mauritius. No address, no entry (unless you can persuade the officers at the airport that you really can't remember the address!).

A yellow fever vaccination certificate is required of travellers over one year of age coming from infected areas.

Customs

Passengers of 16 years and over may bring in 250g (9oz) tobacco, 200 cigarettes or 50 cigars; 2 litres (3½ pints) wine, ale or beer; 1 litre (1¾ pints) spirits; 250ml (9 fl oz) toilet water and up to 100ml (3½ fl oz) perfume.

Animals and plant matter, including flowers and fresh fruit, must have permits before they can be brought into the country. Animals must also undergo a quarantine period. Firearms must be declared on arrival. The importation of drugs results in a death sentence.

Air Travel

The **Sir Seewoosagur Ramgoolam Airport** (tel: 637-3531) is situated at Plaisance, 45km (28 miles) southeast of Port Louis. Air Mauritius has at least one flight daily to Europe, and several flights a week to India, the Far East and southern Africa. It also flies to Réunion (40 minutes) and Rodrigues (90 minutes). There are excellent duty-free shops at the arrival and departure lounges.

Facilities include banks, a post office, bars and a restaurant. Passengers over two years of age pay an airport tax of Rs300 on departure.
Airlines: Air France, South African Airways (both tel: 208-6801) and Air Mauritius (tel: 208-7700) are all in Rogers House, 5 President John Kennedy St, and the British Airways office (tel: 208-1039) is on Duke of Edinburgh Ave, Port Louis.
Air Mauritius Helicopter Services: Bell-Jet Ranger Helicopters operates from selected beach hotels around the island. Trips can be tailored to your requirements, and a commentary is given by the pilot. Full round-the-island tours take about an hour; half-hour trips are also offered. Transfers to and from the airport and your hotel, or between hotels, can be arranged on request (tel: 637-3420, ext 1419).

Regional Sea Links

The modern M.V. *Mauritius Pride* travels twice a month to Rodrigues and other Indian Ocean islands, including Réunion and Madagascar. Freighters travelling in the southwest Indian Ocean are also able to take a limited number of passengers. Contact Rogers House, Port Louis (tel: 208-6801), or Concorde Travel and Tours (*see* p. 122).

Road Travel

An 1800km (1125 mile) network of tarred roads criss-crosses the island. Most roads are in excellent condition, having been resurfaced in 1993/1994. The highway now runs from Plaisance past the plateau towns to the Port Louis harbourside, and from there via Mapou to Grand Baie. Roads tend to be narrow, which can be problematic in built-up areas. Constant hooting is a characteristic feature of driving in Mauritius.
Driver's licence: A valid licence issued in your country of residence can be used in Mauritius. You are not obliged to carry it, although it is advisable to do so in case you do run into problems.
Road rules and signs: Driving is on the left, giving way to the right. The speed limit is 50kph (31mph) in town and 80kph (50mph) in the countryside. It is compulsory to wear a seat belt. Road signs leave a lot to be desired; in fact they are rather quaint (and confusing!), with some carrying distances in miles and some in kilometres. Route numbers, marked on many maps, often don't feature on road signs. It's handy to know the names of neighbouring towns too as not all towns are signposted regularly.
Maps: The Globetrotter Travel Map is a comprehensive, double-sided map; the entire island, showing roads, towns and tourist attractions, is shown on one side, while the reverse side is given over to street plans and detailed maps of popular tourist areas as well as basic maps of Rodrigues and Réunion. The French IGN and English Macmillan maps are both good alternatives.
Petrol: Most filling stations close at 19:00; in Rose Hill the Esso station is open 24 hours a day. Attendants will fill the tank, and do not expect tips. Credit cards are accepted by many filling stations which usually display the Visa and MasterCard logos.
Car hire: To hire a car you must be at least 23 years old and in possession of a valid driver's licence. Major car hire firms such as Avis, Europcar and Hertz are well represented at the larger hotels, but it's worth hunting around the smaller hire companies for cheaper rates. There is a wide range of cars available for hire, from beach-oriented Mini-mokes to more luxurious saloons which can be hired with or without a chauffeur. In case of break-downs, call the hire agency and they should replace the car; insurance is generally covered in the hire price.
Bus service: A bus network covers the entire island. Operating hours are 05:30-20:00 in towns and 06:30-18:30 between villages. A night service runs until 23:00 between Port Louis and Curepipe via Rose Hill, Quatre Bornes and Vacoas. Avoid the rush-hour crush (7:30-9:30 and 16:00-17:30). Fares are cheap and some services very slow. Timetables are available from the National Transport Authority, Victoria Square, and the MTPA, both in Port Louis, or at the airport.
Taxis: Most taxis are not luxurious, and have seen several years' service. Identify

them by their numberplates, which have black lettering on a white background.

There is an official tariff specifying rates per kilometre (including return to the starting point) and per waiting time of 15 minutes. Meters are often not used, even though this is a legal requirement; instead there are standard fares for standard distances, so negotiate before setting out. The information desk at the airport and most hotels will be able to advise how much you should pay for where you want to go. Some taxi drivers are cheaper if you hire them on a daily basis, or better still, for a few days. They are happy to take you all over the island and wait while you see the sights, and some will willingly act as guides. Agree on tariffs before departure, though.

Be wary of asking your taxi-driver's advice on the best places to buy souvenirs or eat: some make deals with shop and restaurant owners whereby they get a commission for bringing in tourists; you may land up missing out or getting ripped off because of this.

Taxi-trains or **share-taxis:** see p. 24.

Mopeds: For hire in the north coast area, mopeds are a cheap and easy way of getting around. Check how long the hire period is (per day or per 24 hours), and make sure you get a helmet with the bike – this is a legal requirement.

Bicycles: These can be hired from most hotels, some tour operators in Grand Baie, and at Péreybère beach.

Clothes: What to Pack

Beach wear and light, cotton casual wear are sensible for daytime. Remember to bring sunglasses, as the glare from both water and sand can be fierce. It's also a good idea to pack a pair of shoes that can be worn in the water to protect your feet from coral, sea urchins and stonefish. Though topless bathing is the norm at many of the international hotels, it is not always well accepted on public beaches.

Light woollens may be needed for cool evenings between June and September. At dusk in summer, cover up to prevent mosquito bites (and/or use a mosquito repellant). In the evening women dress more elegantly in the international hotels, although suits and ties are rarely seen here. Tourists should dress decently in public, especially if planning to visit places of worship.

Money Matters

The monetary unit is the Mauritian rupee (Rs) which is divided into 100 cents. Notes come in denominations of Rs5, 10, 50, 100, 200, 500 and 1000. Coins are available in 5, 10, 20, 25 and 50 cents, Rs1, Rs5. Some old coins remain in circulation, which can be very confusing at times; in particular, the old Rs1 coin, still in use, is only slightly smaller than the new Rs5 coin, and they can easily be mistaken for each other. A few of the coins bear the queen's head as they date back to the time when the island was still a British colony.

Currency restrictions: Visitors are allowed up to Rs700 in notes on arrival and may take out Rs350 when leaving. There is no restriction on the importation of foreign currency in any form such as credit cards, drafts, notes and traveller's cheques.

Credit cards: American Express, Diners, MasterCard and Visa are widely accepted.

Currency exchange: Although you can exchange foreign currency for rupees at all banks and hotels, you can only change rupees back into foreign currency at the airport bank. Keep proof of any exchanges made.

Banks: Towns and some villages have banking facilities. At the airport, banks open according to the arrival and departure of international aircraft. Otherwise, opening hours are 09:30-14:30 from Monday to Friday, and 09:30-12:00 on Saturdays. Holders of Visa and MasterCards can use most automatic tellers, which display the logos of the cards they accept.

Tipping and service charges: Tipping is not generally expected, and is left to your discretion. A government tax surcharge of 10% is added to all hotel and restaurant bills – check whether it is included in the price quoted.

Taxes: General Sales Tax varies from 4.5% to 5%; some traders include GST in the price, others do not. If you are taking advantage of duty-free facilities in the relevant shops, you will need to present your passport and return ticket and pay with a credit card or in foreign currency; you can collect the article at the airport.

Accommodation

Unless otherwise stated, the hotels listed in this book are comfortable, high-quality establishments, with Sun International and Beachcomber groups in particular aimed almost exclusively at the top end of the market; some rank among the best in the world. Mauritius does, however, have accommodation to suit a range of budgets, including modest hotels, self-catering flats and cottages, comfortable guesthouses and pensions. With one or two exceptions in the plateau towns, hotels are usually low-rise developments, often consisting of bungalow-style beachside complexes; major hotels all have one or more restaurants, usually of a high standard. Hotels in the towns are not really geared towards tourists and are of a noticeably lower standard than the beach hotels; rates are also considerably cheaper.

Prices are at their highest over Christmas/New Year and during July/August. When booking at a guesthouse or self-catering accommodation, ask if the sea in front of the accommodation is 'clean', i.e. free of rocks and sea urchins. The majority of hotels have immediate access to good beaches; if not there is sure to be one a short walk away. Find out before booking whether you will have to cross a main road to get to the beach.

Trading Hours

Shops: In the plateau towns and the larger villages, shops are traditionally open from 09:00-18:00 Monday to Wednesday, Friday and Saturday, and 09:00-12:00 on Thursdays. Port Louis shops are open from 09:00-17:00 Monday to Friday, and 09:00-12:00 on weekends. Markets operate between 06:00 and 18:00 from Monday to Saturday, and from 06:00-12.00 on Sundays. However, laws governing trading hours have recently been amended, and Sunday trading is now more widespread. The Continent shopping centre at Phoenix is open until 20:30 every day except Sundays (and until 22:00 on Fridays).

Offices: In the public sector, these are open between 09:00 and 16:00 Monday to Friday and 09:00-12:00 on Saturdays.

Post offices: There are branches of the post office in all towns and villages and at the airport. Opening hours are 08:00-11:15 and 12:00-16:00 Monday to Friday, and 08:00-11:45 on Saturdays.

Pharmacies: From Monday to Saturday, pharmacies are open from 09:00-18:00. A few emergency chemists are open on Sundays – check the newspaper or town hall noticeboards for details.

Measurements

Mauritians are equally comfortable using imperial and metric measurements. You could, for example, be quoted the price of a fish in kilograms, and then have it weighed in pounds! Roadside distance markers are represented in kilometres or miles at random.

Language

English is the official language but French and Creole predominate in everyday life. Various Oriental languages are also spoken.

Communications

Telephones: Public phone booths are becoming common in Mauritius. They are all listed in the telephone directory, but if you cannot locate one, try a post office or Mauritius Telecom offices (the Telecom Tower can be found in Port Louis). The international dialling code for Mauritius and Rodrigues is (230); to call Rodrigues from Mauritius, dial (095) before the individual telephone number. There are no codes within either island. To make an international call from Mauritius, dial 00, then the country code, area code and the number. The local directory enquiries number is 90; for international directory enquiries call 10090.

Mail: It is advisable to post letters at your hotel or a post office; collections elsewhere can be somewhat erratic.

Newspapers: A free press exists in Mauritius. Of the seven daily newspapers, only one, *The Express*, is partly in English. Several overseas newspapers are available at selected outlets but they are usually two or three days old by the time they reach the shops.

Radio/TV: Broadcasts feature mainly French programmes, with a few in English as well as Hindi and other Oriental languages. Satellite television is now available, although limited. Bring a short-wave radio if you wish to hear international broadcasts.

Time

Mauritius time is Greenwich Mean Time plus four hours, three hours ahead of Central European time and two hours ahead of South African time.

Electricity

Power supply throughout the island is 220 volts. Three-pin British-type plugs and two-pin French-type plugs are found in use all over the island.

Water

Water is treated chemically in Mauritius, and is safe to drink. During or after a cyclone, when supplies may have been disrupted, however, it is advisable to drink bottled or boiled water; bottled water is widely available. Water in Rodrigues is not chemically treated and you should always drink bottled water there.

Cyclones

A cyclone is basically a concentration of strong winds. In Mauritius cyclones can reach 280kph (175mph) or more (*see* p. 9), and are usually accompanied by downpours.

The Mauritian Meteorological services are very mindful of the potential damage to the island: they chart the course of each cyclone closely and give out warnings over the radio to the public, assessing the danger. Warning 1 indicates minimal risk. Warning 2 is slightly stronger: hotels are advised to remove boats from the water or risk not being covered by insurance. Warning 3 warns drivers to stay off the roads, failing which they will not be covered by insurance; you should also stock up on candles and food to last two or three days, and store drinking water in case water supplies are affected. Warning 4 indicates that the cyclone is upon the island. Even this is not as doom-laden as it sounds as cyclones can veer away at any time.

Weather patterns are very changeable when a cyclone is nearby. The sea may be calm at one point and very rough at another. Squalls with intermittent bursts of sunshine are common near the sea.

Books

Marine Molluscs of Mauritius and *Birds of Mauritius* by Claude Michel, *Coquillages de la Réunion et de l'île Maurice* by Jean Orinas and Maurice Joy, and *Fleurs et Plantes de la Réunion et de l'île Maurice* by T. Cadet are all useful field guides; *Dive Sites of Mauritius* by Alan Mountain is an excellent and comprehensive guide for divers and snorkellers; *Golden Bats and Pink Pigeons* by Gerald Durrell and the chapter 'Rare, or Medium Rare?' from *Last Chance to See...* by Douglas Adams and Mark Carwardine both give fascinating and amusing insights into the state of conservation on Mauritius.

Medical Services

Most hotels have a medical service or can call a doctor on your behalf. Otherwise there are eight private clinics on the islands and four public hospitals, listed at the front of the telephone directory. The private clinics are preferable.

There are many well-stocked pharmacies on the island (*see* Trading Hours, p. 125).

Health Hazards

Mauritius is fortunate in being relatively free of tropical diseases and poisonous animals (for dangers in the water, *see* p. 33). Don't underestimate the harm and discomfort over-exposure to the sun can cause, however – there's nothing like a bad sunburn on the first day of your visit to ruin your holiday! Always wear a suntan lotion with a high sun protection factor (SPF), especially if you have fair skin.

Useful Contacts

Mauritius Chamber of Commerce and Industry has a comprehensive list of accommodation and prices; 3 Royal St, Port Louis (tel: 208-3301); there is also a counter at the airport.

Conservator of Forests, for permission to visit offshore islands and mountain nature reserves; Botanical Gardens St, Curepipe (tel: 675-4966).

Airport: 637-3531.

Weather: 96.

Emergencies (police/fire/ambulance): 999.